"AND PEOPLE WONDER WHY WE ARE HERE"

A medical student writes:

"I gave 'medical advice' earlier this week to a father, whose son had an abscess on his chest. I told them to take the kids to a doctor. The father thanked me and kissed my hand. I was embarrassed and didn't know what to do, so I kissed his hand."

A Freedom School teacher writes:

"Every class is beautiful. The girls respond, respond, respond. . . They are a sharp group. But they are under-educated and starved for knowledge. They know they have been cheated and they want anything and everything that we can give them."

A get-out-the-vote volunteer writes:

"Fifty times a day people come up to us and thank us and tell us what we're doing is so fine, so good. The kids, playing with boards in the dust, have the greatest smiles. When we're out going from door to door to get people to register, we see a kid get up and run inside. 'There they is' we hear. We are 'they' and everyone knows who 'they' is."

AND A SCARED KID WRITES:

"Yesterday while the Mississippi River was being dragged looking for the three missing civil rights workers, two bodies of Negroes were found—one cut in half and one without a head. Mississippi is the only state where you can drag a river any time and find bodies you were not expecting.

"AND PEOPLE WONDER WHY WE ARE HERE!"

Other SIGNET and MENTOR Books on Race Relations

BLACK LIKE ME *by John Howard Griffin*

The startling, penetrating, first-hand account of a white man who learned what it is like to live as a Negro in the South. Winner of the *Saturday Review* Anisfield-Wolf Award. (#P2709—60¢)

THE TROUBLESOME PRESENCE
by Eli Ginzberg and Alfred S. Eichner

The background of "sit-ins," "kneel-downs," and "freedom rides" in a comprehensive history of the Negro's struggle for equality. (#MT667—75¢)

THE NEGRO REVOLT *by Louis E. Lomax*

A Negro writer's blunt, brilliant report on the current racial unrest in America. (#T2273—75¢)

WHY WE CAN'T WAIT *by Martin Luther King, Jr.*

One of the most eloquent spokesmen for the American Negro reveals the forces, pressures, and implications behind today's quest for civil rights. (#P2476—60¢)

TO OUR READERS: If your dealer does not have the SIGNET and MENTOR books you want, you may order them by mail enclosing the list price plus 10¢ a copy to cover mailing. (New York City residents add 5% Sales Tax. Other New York State residents add 2% plus any local sales or use taxes.) If you would like our free catalog, please request it by postcard. The New American Library, Inc., P. O. Box 2310, Grand Central Station, New York, N. Y. 10017.

Letters

from

MISSISSIPPI

Edited by
ELIZABETH SUTHERLAND
Preface by James W. Silver

A SIGNET BOOK

Published by The New American Library

Excerpts from letters by Geoffrey and Paul Cowan are reprinted by permission of *Esquire* Magazine © 1964 by Esquire, Inc.

SIGNET TRADEMARK REG. U.S. PAT. OFF. AND FOREIGN COUNTRIES
REGISTERED TRADEMARK—MARCA REGISTRADA
HECHO EN CHICAGO, U.S.A.

SIGNET BOOKS are published by
The New American Library, Inc.
1301 Avenue of the Americas, New York, New York 10019

PRINTED IN THE UNITED STATES OF AMERICA

For
Andrew Goodman, twenty
James Chaney, twenty-one
Michael Schwerner, twenty-four

Editor's Note

This book has been prepared with the kind cooperation of the Mississippi Project Parents' Committee, which originally arranged for its publication and collected most of the letters included here.

The editor wishes to thank the many volunteers as well as their parents and friends who made letters available for this book, with the hope that those who do not find their letters here will appreciate the problem of limited space. It should also be noted that letters have been edited for length and sometimes for clarity; such changes are generally indicated by the usual means, but when the changes were inconsequential or when an excess of brackets and dots would have diminished the book's readability, editorial revisions have not been noted. Odd phrasings or inconsistent spellings are intentional; they repeat the language of the original letters. Throughout the book, when volunteers are identified it is by first name only. A complete listing of the full names of those who submitted letters appears at the end of the book.

The editor is grateful to Miss Betty Garman and others of the Student Nonviolent Coordinating Committee for their help. And finally a special word for Tessa, age eleven, who endured many lonely hours and TV dinners while this book was in the making. She understands about Mississippi.

Contents

Preface

In 1856 Walt Whitman asked the slave holders what they would do with Kansas if they got it. "Then would the melt begin," he wrote, "that would not cool till Kansas should be redeemed, as of course it would be." In Mississippi in the summer of 1964 the melt began that will not cool until all citizens in the Magnolia state have their basic American rights.

The signs of the impending collapse of the old order are there for those who can read them. Some fifty Negro first graders are now attending previously all white schools. Negro enrollment at the University of Mississippi has increased one hundred per cent—from one to two—without further violence. In the larger cities the accommodation provisions of the 1964 Civil Rights Law are being partially enforced. Perhaps a couple of thousand new colored registrants have been added to the voting polls of the state. The Mississippi Freedom Democratic Party won an exciting propaganda victory in the Atlantic City convention, masterfully outpointing the state's white political leadership.

But the most devastating affront to the old order, the most momentous challenge to the prevailing caste system, has been the fact of nearly a thousand white summer visitors living and working amiably with Negro families. This major fracture of the established code, along with token desegregation of schools and public accommodations, spells the doom and failure of the Citizens Councils which, ironically, are expanding nationally at the very time they have received their death blow at home.

For the most part, the revolution that is taking place in the closed society has been inspired and implemented from the outside; otherwise, it would have been overwhelmed at birth. It is this massive assault from the country as a whole—the Justice Department, the Congress, the Civil Rights organizations, the church groups, and particularly tens of thousands of individuals who no longer are willing to tolerate Mississippi's nullification of the Constitution that assures the Americanization of almost a million black Mississippians. A most essential ingredient in the rebellion has been the small but increasing indigenous Negro leadership, aided and abetted by conscience-stricken whites beginning to break the shackles of fear.

This is not to say that the revolution will be accomplished in less than a decade or that it will be accomplished at all without continued pressure from the outside. Voluntary compliance with the inevitable is at a minimum in a state whose people are masters of double talk, subterfuge and chicanery and who are accustomed to fierce resistance to change. On the other hand, many industrial leaders, some educators, the most enlightened churchmen, and even a handful of professional men, are beginning to act in accordance with the future. On the whole the politicians have learned nothing or, if they have, are afraid to admit it. It is true that the present governor is a very paragon of virtue and statesmanship in comparison with his stubborn predecessor, and that the mayor of Jackson has moved a long ways from his demagogic conduct of a year ago. But the state legislators, most local officials, the bureaucracy in general, and the myopic columnists of the Jackson newspapers, still chant their hymns of allegiance to the good old days when the Negro knew his place.

The noisemakers of press and politics have all summer long hysterically branded the civil rights "invaders and agitators" as one of a kind, frustrated and immoral females, Communist agents and dupes, unclean do-gooders, and trouble makers. As the letters in this volume indicate, Mississippians have once more been victimized by their leaders. In reality the summer workers were highly disciplined, superbly courageous, extremely intelligent, indefatigable idealists who would not be turned aside by threats of violence or by violence itself. Sons and daughters of corporation executives, of reputable lawyers and physicians, of nationally known politicians and educators, and even the children of owners of factories and industrial plants in Mississippi (as well, of course, as members of hundreds of plain American families), gave the lie to those who tried to downgrade the caliber of youngsters willing to risk their lives for a cause. The cause was nothing more nor less than the implementation of the promise of democracy in the Declaration of Independence and the Constitution of the United States.

Whatever the immediate impact of these crusaders, they have begun the melt which will not cool until second and third class citizenship in Mississippi has gone the way of slavery.

James W. Silver

Letters

from

MISSISSIPPI

● LOCATION OF MISSISSIPPI PROJECTS

And that freedom train's a-comin', comin', comin'
And that freedom train's a-comin', comin', comin'
And that freedom train's a-comin', comin', comin'
Get on board.

It'll be bringing nothing but freedom, freedom, freedom
It'll be bringing nothing but freedom, freedom, freedom
It'll be bringing nothing but freedom, freedom, freedom
Get on board.

They'll be coming by the thousand, thousand, thousand
They'll be coming by the thousand, thousand, thousand
They'll be coming by the thousand, thousand, thousand
Get on board.

1 / The Road to Mississippi

They were called "the volunteers": 650 young people, mostly Northerners and mostly white and mostly students. They were the largest single group of the many people who went to Mississippi in the summer of 1964. They were the nonprofessionals. The kids. And they wrote the letters that make up this book.

Most of them knew why they wanted to go to Mississippi before they left home or school to join the project. Some found out at the orientation sessions held in Ohio, Tennessee and other nearby states. Some learned the best reasons in Mississippi itself. And perhaps a few understood only when they had left.

All of them realized that the eyes of the nation were fixed upon their undertaking: from almost every side came the voices of skepticism as well as admiration. Hostility was not limited to white Mississippians like Mayor Allen Thompson of Jackson, who stood ready to greet the "invaders" with his specially built tank and riot squads. A Louis Harris public opinion poll taken in June among Americans across the nation indicated that 65% opposed the Mississippi Summer Project. The doubts and criticisms ranged wide:

Why Mississippi when there is so much racial injustice in their own backyards?

Let Mississippi do its own house cleaning.

Let the government do the job.

13

*They'll just stir up a lot of resentment among the whites
and make matters worse.*

*They are being used to foster violence and thus force
federal intervention.*

They're just doing it for publicity.

*They're wild-eyed radicals, they're naive idealists, they're
beatniks, they're misfits.*

*But some voices said: They are the cream of our youth.
The hope of this nation.*

*The first contingent of volunteers—about 250 strong—
poured in from all parts of the country for orientation at
Western College for Women in Oxford, Ohio during the week-
end of June 13-14. A second orientation period began the
following week when the first group left. The lush, 200-acre
Oxford campus included an oddly symbolic bird sanctuary;
the dormitory rooms were attractive and the modernistic dining hall of glass and wood served unusually good food. In
these surroundings the volunteers spent a week learning how
to avoid being beaten or killed.*

*A hundred facts of Mississippi life were thrown at them one
day, real tear gas another. They learned how the racist Citizens Councils operate, what sort of work they might be doing,
how to talk to a group of threatening whites, how not to dress.
But their first real discovery had little to do with all this.*

Dear Mom and Jo,   Oxford, Ohio, June 14

The reception at Western College was not warm. I was surprised at how unfriendly and unextending people were. Small
groups formed or had been formed and people seemed concerned with "fitting in." I went to bed. Later that day (today)
I went to register. I still felt uncomfortable but attempted to
shake a few hands. (It wasn't too bad.) Some people were
friendly and helpful. Tremendous enthusiasm was generated
when we all began singing after dinner. It was the spiritual
revival type singing and you know how I love that. We all
must have sung for about 2 hours, and the previous in-group-
ing of Negroes and reservedness of whites seemed to disappear—but not really. . . . Maybe we'll be able to at the end
of the summer, but right now we don't know what it is to be
a Negro and even if we did, the Negroes here would not
accept us. It's the old case of having to prove ourselves. In
their eyes we're rich middle or upper-class whites who've
taken off a summer to help the Negro.

Intellectually, I think many of us whites can understand the

14

Negroes' resentment but emotionally we want to be "accepted" at face value. We want this acceptance because this is part of our reason for going down south, i.e., the basic worth of the individual. I've always thought that my relations with Negroes have been fairly honest. I've gone to a predominantly Negro high school and participated in athletics with them. I've gotten to know Negroes in college . . . I haven't gone out of my way to meet them but those I have met I have gotten along well with, if not intimately. What I mean to say is that I never detected a "difference," or an inability to communicate with one another. . . . But what I am finding here is a different situation and perhaps a more honest one . . .

Love,

Lew

June 15

. . . Us white kids here are in a position we've never been in before. The direction of the whole program is under Negro leadership—almost entirely. And a large part of that leadership is young people from the South—Negroes who've had experience just because they're Negroes and because they've been active in the movement. And here "we" are, for the most part never experiencing any injustice other than "No, I won't let you see your exam paper . . ."

Dear Peggy:

. . . All whites who read Baldwin ask, "Is he right? Do they really hate us?" I have never before talked to a Negro about his feelings toward whites. A wonderful Negro man from Detroit named Joe Harrison told me here at Oxford, "I always feel much more comfortable with Negroes than with whites. But I can become good friends with white people."

And one SNCC [Student Nonviolent Coordinating Committee] worker—Frank Smith—said, "I grew up hating all white folks. It wasn't till a couple of years ago that I learned that there could be good whites—and even now I sometimes wonder."

So, there is this great reluctance and distrust, born of generations of oppression and slavery . . . It seems that if more whites understood this—especially white liberals—race relations might be a lot less strained.

I have also discovered a lot about my own feelings about race. I grew up in an upper middle-class Westchester home, where my parents were good liberals, but I never knew any

Negroes except the woman who cooked and cleaned for us. I loved her very much and she, me. . . . We all called her "Sarah" while she called me "Ellen" and my parents "Mr. and Mrs."

Consequently, although my parents told me that Negroes were just as good as whites—I must have seen them in the role of servants. Once, my mother tells me, when I was little, we were driving along a road near our house and passed a Negro woman waiting for a bus. "There's somebody's maid," I said.

To arrive in Ohio, where there were 60 or 70 Negro kids my age—all close friends and rather cliquish at first—was a frightening experience. It was not that I looked down on them at all—quite the contrary: I was awed by them. For the first few days, I mostly hung around with the kids from Harvard. I sat with them at meals or in meetings, walking by the groups of Negro kids who also sat together at the table or under a tree on the grass. . . . But as the week wore on, things began to change.

Ellen

The turning point came with the showing of a film, on June 16.

Dearest,

For the first two days there was a noticeable tension between the volunteers and the staff. . . . Then, Tuesday night we saw a movie made by CBS Reports ["Mississippi and the Fifteenth Amendment"] describing how the Negro was discriminated against in Mississippi with regard to voting. Some of the film was absolutely ridiculous and ludicrous—a big, fat, really fat and ugly white county registrar prevents Negroes from voting; the stupid, really completely irrational and dishonest views of some white Southerners and so on. Six of the staff members got up and walked out of the movie because it was so real to them while we laughed because it was so completely foreign to us—if anyone had said what they did in the movie, we in the North would lock them up or dismiss them completely, but this is the way many white Southerners think.

After the movie one of the staff told us why they had walked out and it shook some of us up. We were afraid the whole movement was going to fall apart . . .

Love,
Wally

. . . We had the whole thing out in the living room, with everybody sitting on the floor or standing along the walls. The kids brought out their gripes: the staff was distant, they didn't let us know what was going on or who would be assigned where, or how we would be assigned, and they looked down on us for not having been through what they had. They shouldn't walk out like that, saying in effect you white people are too stupid to understand how serious all of this is.

Other people argued that we should take into account all of the hardships they were going through, and the fact that they had a lot on their minds. Others again demanded that the staff respect us more: we were after all products of *our* environments, and did not understand Mississippi, and had not been beaten. Could we do something really concrete down there, or are we just pawns? If so, why should we go down there indeed? Did the staff trust us, could we learn?

Staff members began drifting in from a meeting and entered the discussion. "We did not walk out because of you, necessarily. We have seen too much of that stuff in the flesh. We know that bastard and don't have to see him on the screen." One guy said "if you get mad at us walking out, just wait until they break your head in, and see if you don't have something to get mad about. Ask Jimmy Travis over there what he thinks about the project. What does he think about Mississippi? He has six slugs in him, man, and the last one went right through the back of his neck when he was driving a car outside Greenwood. Ask Jesse here—he has been beaten so that we couldn't recognize him time and time and time and time again. If you don't get scared, pack up and get the hell out of here because we don't need any favors of people who don't know what they are doing here in the first place."

"We cried over you in the staff meeting because we love you and are afraid for you. We are grown men and women who have been beaten and shot at, and we cried for you. Somebody walked out of a movie, but you won't see anybody walk out on your picket line. When you get beaten up, I am going to be right behind you. The song we sang yesterday was dedicated to a couple of the people now in jail, and they know we are singing and thinking about them. As long as there is one person alive wearing a SNCC pin they know. And you had better know it too, or else get out. I was a good soldier in Korea. I can stick a bayonet in your back in the right spot so that you don't make a sound. I know how to use piano wire around your neck and then let you fall to the

17

ground soft. And all the time in Korea I was sick to the guts because I was being taught to kill so good. Don't tell me that you are coming down to help me because you are saving yourselves. We are proud of you, and love you. Don't worry when we don't have time to shake hands, because that's not the SNCC greeting anyway. We hug and kiss you because we love you."

Here is what I said: people have been talking about Americans, and how there is more than just the black man's problem. Somebody said that we sounded like a sick bunch of people with all of our complaints. Well, we are all sick, black and white, because we are Americans, and that fat bastard on the screen has poisoned all of us. The whole god damn country has gone to hell, and we are the only ones who can save it. Isn't it sick when we have to see an in-group sitting together at lunch and feel that they are suspicious of us because we are white? That is why we are going down, not to help the Negro, but to get rid of those guys for all of us. It is natural that these things should come out, because that bastard put it into all of us. That is why the training is a week long and not just two days . . .

Then some of the staff people came in singing, and we all sang together, and the first time *really* together. The crisis is past, I think.

Love,

Bill

With the tension between Negro staff and white volunteers broken, if not resolved, the volunteers began to see Mississippi through the eyes of those who knew it all too well. Their understanding of what lay ahead grew stronger—as did their fear.

Dear People at home in the Safe, Safe North,   June 17

Mississippi is going to be hell this summer. Monday Jim Forman, executive secretary of SNCC stood up during one of the general sessions and calmly told the staff (who already knew) and the volunteers that they could all expect to be arrested, jailed, and beaten this summer, and, in many cases, shot at. There is a quiet Negro fellow on the staff who has an ugly scar on his neck and another on his shoulder where he stopped .45 slugs. . . . Another fellow told this morning how his father and later his brother had been shot to death. . . . I'd venture to say that every member of the Mississippi staff has been beaten at least once and he who has not been shot

18

at is rare. It is impossible for you to imagine what we are going in to, as it is for me now, but I'm beginning to see . . .

Please talk up Mississippi up North, pass around the materials I am sending, and begin petitioning the Federal government for intervention . . .

Love,

Xtoph

Dear God, also dear me, and anyone else interested,   June 19

I want to write everything down now, while I have time and can and before I leave Oxford. . . .

My feelings are many and mixed and are not always the same. . . . When I began this letter I was feeling quite calm and relaxed, then the butterflies started in the pit of my stomach, they subsided somewhat and then continued to my hands.

Whenever I am scared or terribly excited about something, I have always gotten this feeling in my stomach and then often even in my hands. But this afternoon I felt it so that I ached—my whole stomach, my chest, my arms, hands, legs and even down to my feet. That is pretty nearly all of me. . . .

A Negro girl said to me in the john a few minutes ago that she wondered if I had a match. I said No. And she said "You don't smoke yet?" I replied, "no." "You will before the end of the summer," she said.

She went on to tell me, "I do because I'm nervous. No, I'm going to quit saying I'm nervous. I'm scared. Sometimes I smoke two packs a day."

She also said she had been told that many of the girls, especially in a certain other dorm, cried all by themselves at night, that they really didn't want to go. "If I didn't really want to go I wouldn't go" she said. And I said "Sometimes there isn't a really don't and a really do." She continued, "And sometimes you've told the people back home you were going to help and what will they think if you come home now." I said "Well, that would present a problem too."

Perhaps I should have said "that does present a problem too." I actually have thought about the feelings or thoughts of others should I back out. So this is one of the pressures. But only one, and who can say how large or small . . .

With much love, a very (calm right now) me,

Virginia

Monday night, June 15

I turned down a chance to work in the southwest part of

the state, the most dangerous area. I talked to a staff member covering that area for about fifteen minutes and he told me about the five Negroes who have been taken into the woods and shot in the last three months. . . . I told him that I couldn't go in there because I was just too scared. I felt so bad I was about ready to forget about going to Mississippi at all. But I still wanted to go; I just didn't feel like giving up my life. After thinking about this seeming contradiction, I decided that I have not discovered just how dedicated I am to the civil rights cause and that that is the purpose of the trip. . . .

Amidst the apprehension, the volunteers went on listening and learning. The days were packed from morning to night, the week from beginning to end, with new knowledge and new songs and especially new people.

Dear family and friends,   June 18

Sunday evening, the first program was a solemn memorial service for Medgar Evers conducted by Ed King, a native Mississippian who is Methodist chaplain and dean at Tougaloo —the Negro college outside of Jackson. Monday morning King led off the first session with a run-down of some of the factors which contribute to making Miss. a police state. King is a soft-spoken man with large scars from an auto accident disfiguring one side of his face. He ran for Lieutenant Governor in the Freedom Election run last year by SNCC. He told about the techniques the White Citizens Council, which receives state funds, has used to keep control of the state. No politician can afford to be a moderate. Three were voted out recently for voting against an extreme piece of anti-Negro legislation. In the past six years over 60 Methodist ministers have been forced out of the Southern half of the state alone. Merchants who meet the terms of the civil rights groups are economically coerced to change or leave. All widely read newspapers simply deny the 'white guilt for violence and usually ignore incidents entirely. National news on TV is interrupted by local commercials or by saying, "The following is an example of biased untrue Yankee reporting." King says that he sees how there can be some truth to the contention that many Germans didn't know about the treatment of the Jew under Hitler.

Next Bob Moses talked to us in his quiet, reasoned manner about the project and the situation in various parts of the state. Bob warned us that we are all victims of the plague of prejudice but must not make the mistake that the authorities in Camus' *Plague* made by resisting the recognition of the disease because recognition would have made action necessary. . . . He then sketched some of the goals of the summer. He said that the mere fact of our spending the summer in Negro homes would be a very important victory. It is also hoped that we, through our connections back home will give the project more projection, and bring the Justice Dept. into Mississippi in a bigger way.

In the next session the body was broken down into small groups in which project directors from the local projects described in some detail the conditions in their counties. I happened to be assigned to a group where Charles McLaurin was talking about Sunflower and Bolivar counties. He is a dynamic, clear speaker whose determination, good humor and calmness are massively impressive. These SNCC staff people must really stand out against the background of a lazy dead-end society. It becomes almost understandable how they can persuade people to risk house, job and life to go down and attempt to register.

That evening we went back into the same groups and discussed race relations. This was a painful rather intimate discussion. . . . One boy from West Virginia confessed that he is quite embarrassed when confronted by a group of Negroes and asked how he should act. A little blond Smith girl said she knew what he meant though she didn't have the problem herself, in fact she didn't know whether it was environment or heredity but she found Southern Negroes quite attractive. The discussion was very valuable in posing the problem of how does one adapt without selling out his own identity . . .

Tuesday we had more regional briefings. Then there was an informal general session to discuss various problems. The most interesting discussion was about how we should confront the white kids in Mississippi who want to talk to us and persuade us to go back home. Should we insist that a Negro come along. If their minds are closed what is the use of talking to them. . . . On the other hand it is so important, I feel, to get into the white community and let somebody know what we are like. I imagine the rumors about the invasion of Communists are getting pretty wild.

Tuesday evening was a talk by Charles Morgan, the courageous Birmingham attorney who stood up at the time of the bombings and made a strong public statement in favor of sanity. He has since been forced out of Birmingham by economic coercion and published a book, *A Time to Speak*. He warned us gravely about the dangers of Mississippi. Said he thought that atrocities don't soften but harden the local

21

people. . . . He said one thing that might help was that Mississippi is very concerned about its image. He laid the slow movement of the civil rights cause in the South not to the strength of Southern opposition but to the weakness of the North on the issue. . . . He ended by solemnly stating that he admired our courage. From a guy like that who has seen a lot of fire, this was really frightening. We have all lived under the increasing weight of fear and the struggle to come to terms with the possibility of death consumes much of our emotional energy . . .

Just the security precautions are scary: beware of cars without tags—they are always danger; never go out alone; never go out after dark; never be the last out of a mass meeting; watch for cops without their badge; listen for an accelerating car outside; if you wake up at night thinking there is danger, wake everybody up. There seems to be a very good type instinct for preservation. Some of the Negro field secretaries I was talking to informally told how they played like real Uncle Toms to the cops when in danger. . . .

Wednesday, Rev. James Lawson presented and skillfully defended Christian revolutionary nonviolence as a way of life. Most of the staff and volunteers were agnostic nonviolent technicians. The discussion was hot but very real. It became clear that not all nonviolent techniques could be practised by certain personality types. Only perhaps 10% can talk successfully with someone who is going to beat you. For the rest, withdrawal seems the best reaction. . . .

Thursday we got some practical legal counsel from one of three Negro lawyers in Mississippi who takes civil rights cases. He is a wily old fox with a wonderful sense of humor and a great gift for diplomacy (no, not Uncle Tomming). Also heard from head of legal defense fund and others. There will be 150 lawyers in the state this summer! Friday morning we heard John Doar, Burke Marshall's assistant in the Justice Department, talk about what they would be doing there. He said they would keep very close watch on us and try to watch for trouble brewing. However, he said unless there is a Federal court order to bring Federal troops into an area, responsibility for maintaining law and order is left up to the local law enforcement agencies. The kids' questions and statements were quite burning. There is a law which gives the FBI power to arrest and protect people from intimidation of their right to vote. . . .

Love,

Mike

P.S. A word about the group. A surprising number of young married couples. One school teacher who left wife and kids at home. Maybe a majority of Young Democrat types with a good representation of people from the left. It is hard to tell how we will turn out till we have seen action.

Dear Folks,

A great deal of tension and a great deal of camaraderie here at Oxford. Workshops and role-playing are constant. We staged one situation, a screaming mob lining the steps to the courthouse while a small band of registrants tried to get through. The inevitable happened—what will actually happen in Mississippi happened. The chanting mob (instructed to be as brutal as possible, and to pull no punches) turned into a clawing, pounding mob, and we volunteer registrants were down in our crouched-up ball. Casualties? A couple of scratches, a sprained ankle, and one cameraman who got swept up was a little bit shaken. It seems like brutal play, and it is. We've got to be ready for anything, and we must prepare for it ourselves. Once we get south we are nonviolent; we must get whatever there is in our systems out now, and we must also learn to take the worst. Some of the staff members walk around carrying sections of hose. This strangely terrible training in brutality may well save lives. (I must confess, I have not been able to take part in even the screaming of a mob scene, much less the pummeling. Wherever possible, I am among the victims.)

We have registration workshops, too. And lecturers came from all over the country to speak to us. And we sing. What "We Shall Overcome" is to the national movement, "We'll never turn back" is to the Mississippi workers. It is a slow song, measured out in grief and determination. The final verse goes,

> We have hung our head and cried,
> Cried for those like Lee*
> who died
> Died for you and died for me,
> Died for the cause of equality,
> But we will never turn back
> Until we've all been free
> And we have equality, and we have equality.

Love,

Jim

*Herbert Lee, Negro voter registration worker killed in Liberty, Miss., in 1961.

Dear Mom and Dad,

A lot of the meetings have been run by a Negro Mennonite minister from Georgia, a member of the National Council of Churches. (The NCC is paying for this orientation, and has some excellent staff people here.) His name is Vincent Harding, plump, bespectacled, a brilliant moderator in discussions because he reacts so honestly and humorously to every question. Yesterday he gave a long talk about people using each other and where to watch out for this within the movement itself (Negro man accuses white girl of being a racist if she won't go to bed with him, or vice versa; or white girl looking for "my summer Negro"; or Negroes in the community using volunteers as the only available victims of their suppressed hostility to whites in general, etc., etc.). These are examples of the kind of honesty that characterizes the whole training session. His main point was that people within the movement must not use each other because it is that very exploitation of someone else, which turns him from a human being into an object, that the movement is fighting against.

Love,
Susan

Dear John and Cleo,

. . . I feel such a need for you and really crave to somehow have you experiencing what is important to me. So look, please, at the enclosed material.

In the *Student Voice*, look especially at Mrs. Hamer's face. . . . She was a timekeeper on a cotton plantation. When she registered to vote she was fired from a job she had held for 18 years and made to leave the plantation. Soon her husband, who had been there about 30 years was also fired. In the course of her work for civil rights which followed, she was jailed. Her jailors brought in black prisoners to beat her. One of the black men's hips had been so thrown out of joint that it was jutting out several inches. He and his fellows had been given corn liquor. He was told that if they didn't beat her his other hip would be thrown out . . . To watch her limp around here, encouraging the prayer sessions in which we remember Sen. Eastland and Gov. Johnson and all the brutal people they sanction, is almost too much to take. But it's also a never-failing source of courage and determination. . . .

Does America really know about these people and these places and about incidents of terror that occur every day? I didn't really. And I still don't sometimes. And I expect that

even you really don't. As Robert Moses told us: When you're
not in Mississippi, it's not real and when you're there the rest
of the world isn't real . . .

Love,

Jo

The people here, most particularly the top-level directors
of the entire project, are impressive. They are wise, caring,
courageous, honest, and full of love. All those adjectives in a
list don't mean much. The point is, I trust them and believe
in them not only more than I expected to, but more than I
trust any other group organizers I can think of. The director
of the Summer Project, as you probably know, is Bob Moses.
He is about thirty, married to a Negro girl, comes, I think,
from New York, but has been a SNCC staff worker in Miss.
for some time. He is a careful thinker, expresses himself with
great economy and honesty, and with every word one is amazed
at the amount of caring in the man. He is more or less the
Jesus of the whole project, not because he asks to be, but because of everyone's reaction to him. (I forgot to say, he's a
Negro.) He has a very intelligent face, wears glasses, blue
denim overalls. . . .

June 18

. . . he was not in the least dynamic, but he forced you
by what he said and by his manner of saying it, to want to
partake of him, to come to him. He was not in any way out-
going, yet when he spoke you felt close to him.

Dear Lynne,

The organization here is a real student movement. And it
looks like it will be around a long time. I would not be surprised if it really does, with time, influence the course of
American history through the leaders it produces and develops
—for that is one of its main objectives. . . . The savvy of the
organization is a marvel. It is shrewd, calculating, and geared
for years of struggle. Its members . . . have the strange ability to discuss, plan, scheme, openly and honestly disagree, and
then come to a definite decision which all follow. . . .

Now these people are only students. They are taking on a
state and perhaps a nation which they think has ignored the
heritage of the United States and has violated the fundamental
rights of man. They have acted when few others would. They
are speaking about a festering sore in this nation. The people
who are bugged by this are responding. The sore is not just

segregation but the general de-humanization of American life . . .

Right now the church and Christians are politically impotent. Unless they do something soon, they will become more and more so, until they are snuffed out. That is why to peel off the layers of do-nothing spiritualists, apathetic worshippers, navel-gazers, and to institute people who will make a sacrifice, a radical . . . witness for comfort and "happiness" is imperative for the church . . .

Love,
Dave

Dear Mom and Dad,

. . . I had no idea that so many young people of the age and education of the people here had any serious commitment to religion in this country. It is disturbing, and reassuring. Disturbing, because I'm afraid the faith of some of these nice little girls may run into difficulties if things start happening. Reassuring, because if it survives or already has survived such things, it will be a mighty stay for those of us whose commitment is mostly intellectual. . . .

Love,
Gene

. . . These people—the Mississippians and the SNCC staff members—are the ones who are really free. More free, certainly, than the Southern white imprisoned in his hatred for the Negro. Maybe you have to see the people's faces, hear them talk and sing and struggle, to understand the Movement. You should—you must—understand this Movement, for it is the most important thing involving people in America today . . .

Dear folks, June 21

. . . One sees a freedom here that is so much more than just the ironical fact that the enslaved people are, at least relatively, the liberated ones. Some "white" people sit at their feet wondering at this sorrow freed and made beautiful, sensing dimly in themselves a similar pain but knowing, dimly, that they have bound and frustrated it by their fear of it. . . . I think what is at the root of what I experienced today with these black people was a sense of tragedy. And I mustn't forget how joy and deep humor are involved in that sense, how they are all one and how that is why it *is* the key. If we

26

realize that safety is a myth, aren't we in a sense "saved" by that knowledge and acceptance of death?

. . . I begin to realize that it is a war that I will enter and that the enemy is even lunatic, even driven into frenzy by his fear. But I also learn that the enemy is very much myself and all of America and, perhaps, of humanity. . . . I cannot agree with that "sympathetic" American who from his "safe" and carefully maintained distance says that we must slow up, that we must not push. I suspect this attitude, as I suspect that part of it which I see in myself, because it says that something abnormal and therefore ominous, a naked reality, is drawing too close and threatening the sacred status quo. I think that there is too much piety and wise head-shaking about "Mississippi". . . . Has everybody in the U.S. asked himself—asked himself!—am I prejudiced? asked himself persistently until he arrives at that prejudice that is inevitably there by the nature of our society?

Love,

Bret

While the volunteers searched their minds and hearts, the outside world watched. The volunteers were half glad that national attention had been focused on the project, half angry at the kind of attention. . . .

Dear people,

All around the campus swarm reporters and photographers. Claude Sitton is here from *The New York Times;* Karl Fleming from *Newsweek;* Mrs. Homer Bigart from CBS; Dick Cunningham from the Minneapolis *Tribune;* Nick von Hoffman from the Chicago Daily *News.* They are not here to watch the SNCC staff; as Bob Moses said in a speech the first morning, the press is interested in the students, not the staff, and not the people of Mississippi. . . . *Look* Magazine is searching for the ideal naive northern middle-class white girl. For the national press, that's the big story. And when one of us gets killed, the story will be even bigger.

But the big story out of Mississippi this summer ought not to be about my participation in the movement, or even my death. The big story ought to be Life in Mississippi. If that life is ugly, then its creators must be villains, and those who endure must be beautiful. . . . The purpose of this summer's program is to spotlight oppressed Mississippi; if northern college students dominate the spotlight, the project will, in large measure, have failed.

Geoff

Not only wrong emphasis troubled the volunteers, but also the attacks and inaccuracies. They answered the many naysayers with logic or anger or the truth of their own observations.

. . . Not one of us northern volunteers would deny the existence of oppressive systems in the North—especially in the city slums. . . . But it is stronger and more oppressive in Mississippi. Another thing—Mississippi is just a start—this whole country needs changing so that everyone can live a life in which he is able to realize his full capacities as a human being. Perhaps the reason we are going to Mississippi rather than New York or Philadelphia or even Seattle or Minneapolis is that here is an organized program through which we can use our skills and our lives to bring some measure of justice, maybe even love, to this state and the rest of the country.

One other question—from my point of view the most important and at the same time, the most disturbing—is why not leave the whole problem to the Federal Government? . . . The federal government is not doing the work that needs to be done to change Mississippi. This very question, though, is a reflection of the whole country's attitude of let someone else do it. . . .

Dear Al,   June 29

As you expressed in your letter, you and your law partners believe the effects of outsiders coming into Mississippi will be negative and a great amount of resentment will build up (only to be released by violence—my parenthesis). I cannot deny the fact that some resentment has developed in the *white* community—but our purpose is to work and develop the *Negro* community. . . .

As far as changing the white folks, I've already expressed my doubts about what can be accomplished. These folks have deeply entrenched values about a certain way of life. But you and I both know the effect which enforced law has upon changing people. . . . The major fault so far is that the laws have not been enforced, especially in the south, and more subtly in the north . . .

Best,

Lew

Dear Mr. M.:

A letter from you to Miss Sharon Anderson was read over

the loudspeaker in our dining room at the Mississippi project orientation sessions at the Western College for Women. Some found it amusing. Some found it disgusting. I did not find it amusing . . .

You say among other things that this Mississippi project should be left to experts. What experts? Experts like you? Experts have done nothing for three hundred years. Many Negro people in Mississippi are no better off than they were in the days of slavery. Furthermore, did Jesus Christ say, "Let the experts preach the gospel?" No! He commanded everyone who loves Him to "take up thy cross and follow me." Christ said to love one's neighbor. And do you remember that a lawyer tried to trick Christ by asking, "Who is my neighbor?" And what did Jesus answer? He told the story of the Good Samaritan. Many people are our neighbors. But especially, our neighbor is a person of a different race.

You are quite right that there is plenty to do in the field of race relations right in our own back yard. That's one of the favorite excuses of those who don't want anything done. I have done a great deal in my own back yard, which is New York City. I have helped Negroes to get a decent apartment which was denied them merely because they were Negroes. I have helped get five-day trash collection on some streets in the Negro ghetto area of Brooklyn. I have helped break down the hiring discrimination practiced in New York City. There is still much to be done. But that in no way alleviates anything that must be done in Mississippi. . . .

Suppose you had lived at the time of the French Revolution. Which side would you have been on? Or suppose you had lived at the time of the American Revolution? Which side would you have been on? Of course we can easily say nowadays which side we would have been on because those battles have been fought and won so that it's now perfectly safe to take sides. But there is a battle to be won now today. . . . Has it ever occurred to you that George Washington was a criminal at the time that he fought the Revolution? Of course he was. . . . His army was a bunch of rabble-rousers. Isn't that always the way? Yesterday's fools are tomorrow's heroes —that is, if they win. Well, we intend to win. And while we're winning, you'll sit on your comfortable hind parts and tell me that we're doing it all wrong. . . .

What are you afraid of? Are you afraid that your position in society is so precarious that if anyone rocks the boat, you'll fall in and drown? What a pity! If I live to be 76 years old, I hope that I will have become more intelligent than I am now, not less. You may call me a naive, white college student. . . .

It might be that some of us are naive. But you ought to praise God that they can do what they're doing in spite of their naivete. Did you ever do any such thing when you were their age? Maybe that's why you resent their doing this great thing . . .

But, Mr. M., it's not too late even at 76. . . . Your body might be too old to run with a teen-ager but the wisdom of a person of your years should enable you to have ideas that can run ahead of all these eager youths. Please, Mr. M., don't sit beside the road of life and moan and groan because the younger generation is passing you by. Get up and run!

Sincerely,

Than R.P.

And then the volunteers had their own families to contend with. The grandmother of one student had written to the boy's father: "I do not understand what he is trying to do in Mississippi. I hope he finds something pleasant and what he wants. Mississippi never sounded interesting to me."

Some parents were sympathetic. But many were uncomprehending, others were simply afraid for their children. Thus a number of volunteers had gone to Oxford secretly. Or against the wishes of their families. They tried to explain.

Dear Dad,   June 24

By now you know that what I told you about my plans for the summer was in part a deliberate lie. I'm sorry about this. I thought it was a necessary evil at the time but now I wish I had faced you and told you what I was up to.

The trip through the south was genuine . . . We saw almost every battle-field in the south, in addition to New Orleans, a few Georgia beaches and a grand old plantation outside Natchez, Miss.

Now the trip is over. I am at the orientation session for the "Mississippi Summer Project" with the Student Nonviolent Coordinating Committee (we are called "Snick" for SNCC, kind of a rotten name).

. . . I am sure that you are convinced that I have fallen in with agitators and a dangerous brand of screwballs. Well for some time I feared the same thing myself. I have found the facts to be otherwise . . . And there will be no mass demonstrations, there will be no picketing and no sit-ins. We are not even dreaming of total integration this summer and in this decade . . .

I am, of course, living hand to mouth now. I expect that

you are so disgusted with this whole business that you will try to starve me out. You may succeed. I receive no pay from SNCC. If in fact, I have completely misjudged your reaction I would be only too happy—ever grateful indeed—for support.

I will write you once a week. I am sorry if this frightens or saddens you.

Bill

Dear Mom and Dad, June 27

This letter is hard to write because I would like so much to communicate how I feel and I don't know if I can. It is very hard to answer to your attitude that if I loved you I wouldn't do this—hard, because the thought is cruel. I can only hope you have the sensitivity to understand that I can both love you very much *and* desire to go to Mississippi. I have no way of demonstrating my love. It is simply a fact and that is all I can say. . . .

I hope you will accept my decision even if you do not agree with me. There comes a time when you have to do things which your parents do not agree with. . . . Convictions are worthless in themselves. In fact, if they don't become actions, they are worse than worthless—they become a force of evil in themselves. You can't run away from a broadened awareness . . . If you try, it follows you in your conscience, or you become a self-deceiving person who has numbed some of his humanness. I think you have to live to the fullest extent to which you have gained an awareness or you are less than the human being you are capable of being . . . This doesn't apply just to civil rights or social consciousness but to all the experiences of life . . .

Love,
Bonnie

Dear Folks,

Concerning the "practicality" of such a venture: nothing could be more "lucrative," "profitable," than teaching in Mississippi this summer. . . . I want to fulfill myself, not to prove myself. I do not want to spend my life in the pursuit and enjoyment of comfort and security; I want to pursue my spiritual growth. It is all ultimately selfish: I "save" myself by committing myself to the concerns of other men. . . . I want to teach in Negro schools after graduation. The freedom schools could be the most practical kind of preparation for such a career—and of more value than the life I

31

lead at Stanford among the rather insipid and spoilt, ego-centric products of the middle class.

You should know that it would be a lot nicer in Hawaii than in Mississippi this summer. I am afraid of the situation down there, and the beaches and the safety are very alluring. But I am perhaps more afraid of the kind of life I would fall into in Hawaii. I sense somehow that I am at a crucial moment in my life and that to return home where everything is secure and made for me would be to choose a kind of death. I fear the kind of lethargy that I fell into in Munich . . . I feel the urgent need, somehow, to enter life, to be born into it. . . .

Love,
Bret

The time to leave for Mississippi came near. Some of the volunteers tried to catch hold of the week's meaning.

The past week has been, without doubt, the most amazing of my entire life. Now that I've felt what it is to be involved and committed, it seems hard to believe that I could be content with any other kind of life. I've thought about death a lot and what death means about life, and I know that right now I don't want to live any way but the way I am . . .

. . . I wish I could see you for just a few hours to *tell* you what has happened here this week, and what might happen this summer—both inside and outside of me and this environment. It's an intense and frightening but deeply human and both ugly and beautiful world. I think I've never felt so strangely exhausted and exhilarated, scared to death and aching to get down there. . . .

Dear Mom and Dad,

If the rest of the summer is a failure, this week alone will have been enough. Of course there's been a terrific amount of tension and anxiety, but of a constructive kind, by and large, the kind that enables you to understand yourself and what you're doing. Bob Moses said that when no one had dropped out by Wednesday, he was very worried, it didn't seem real. Since then a few have left, but not too many . . .

It's time to go. I know you'll worry, and we will worry with you. In many ways it's harder to be in NY waiting for news than in Miss. doing things . . .

Joe and Nancy

The time for departure is about 24 hours away. The atmosphere here is very tense and yet amazingly calm considering what may lie ahead . . . I find out that I function almost normally (despite what I am prepared to face) except for brief intervals when the situation, with its full implications, suddenly focuses before my eyes.

I hope the Mississippi Summer Project creates a national crisis of a positive nature. This is probably impossible. The press wants blood and that is what you will hear about. . . .

The first bus and carloads of volunteers left for Mississippi on Saturday, June 20, looking like a strange mixture of kids going to camp and soldiers off to war. Others departed the next day. At the same time there were new arrivals and a new week of orientation began.

That Sunday, a volunteer already arrived in Meridian, Miss., sat down to write a letter.

Dear Stark . . .   June 21

Hi. As you said, no picture postcards to be had, or at least not anywhere I've been, so this'll have to do.

They said that Meridian was an easy town. Comparatively speaking, of course, meaning that the police aren't altogether that terrible, and they try to hold down the vigilante types. Right now, tho, we're all sitting here in the office being quietly nervous as hell. This morning Mickey, who's the project director, and Chaney, a local staff member and Andy, who's a volunteer, all went out to one of the rougher rural counties to see about a church that was burned down a few days ago. They said they'd be back by four, and now it's coming on to ten. We've been calling the Jackson office all day, and have checked all the jails around, and they're not in any of them. No word from them of any kind. We've had people out looking for them and they haven't found anything. We've been in touch with the FBI and DJ [Department of Justice] but I don't quite know if they're doing much of anything. Philadelphia, Miss., that's where they went to see about the church. The city of brotherly love. Everywhere you go here, there's hate. Just now when some of us went down the street for coffee, they were followed by a carload of white hoods. Now that we're back inside, there are two carloads of hoods and one carload, no two, of police, following each other around in slow circles outside. Sometimes when the hoods pass they yell something. "White nigger lover" seems to be a favorite. I wish I knew more what the intentions of the police are. In this town, they probably are trying to keep the hoods from shooting us or something, but it's hard to tell. It's funny, you know, to come from a place where the police are expected to protect you into one where either you're not sure or else you know very well they're against you.

Still no word from the missing people. It must be 11 by now. No one has really said anything about the kinds of things that we're all thinking could have happened to them. The people who've been out looking just came back. Now we talk about the Klan. The FBI is trying to find some grounds to get into the case full strength. Wish they'd hurry up about it.

Hot here, down to 95 now in the office, which is an improvement. Everyone now is very quiet, just sitting, and watching out of the darkened windows a little bit, watching the cars that circle. There's a couple of people standing around on the corner. One of them is a little kid who gets the license number of the circling cars. Besides that, there's nothing out there, just a kind of brightly lit street, with the electric wires crisscrossing in front of the window, and the darkness behind you when you sit in the window. Nothing to do but play pingpong or read and wait for the phone to ring. I've been reading *All Quiet on the Western Front*. Somehow it's appropriate, or maybe not. We'll see . . .

Love,
Edna

At Oxford, on Monday morning, Mrs. Rita Schwerner announced to the new group of volunteers that her husband Michael was missing in Philadelphia together with James Chaney and Andrew Goodman, a New Yorker who had just arrived after attending the first orientation session.

The volunteers rushed to wire or call their Congressmen and demand federal protection for civil rights workers in Mississippi. There was little else to do about the disappearance except wait for news. And think, or write . . .

Dear Mom and Dad,

I cannot begin to tell you how it feels to be here. . . . knowing about them. You feel like it couldn't be real. No—uh-*huh*. They were in Oxford only a few days before—they couldn't already be in such danger. But then all of a sudden—the disbelief is countered by a vivid picture of reality—that it could be you. And then there's this weird feeling of guilt because it wasn't you—and here you are on a beautiful campus trying so hard to understand just what danger is anyway. Everyone suspects the worse to have happened to the men but no one says anything . . .

A lot of kids are trying to be real casual and cool and funny about everything so they don't worry their folks. This seems silly to me—especially with you—because you're in this with us in the sense that unlike a lot of parents—you realize the significance of this summer as much as I do. . . .

Love,

Barbara

Dear Dad,   June 24

The mood up here [in Oxford, Ohio] is, of course, very strained with those three guys who disappeared Sunday, dead, most likely. Saturday night, I ate dinner with the wife of one of them. She was telling me about all the great things she and her husband were working on. She looks younger than me. What does she do now? Give up the movement? What a terrible rotten life this is! I feel that the only meaningful type of work is the Movement but I don't want myself or anyone I've met to have to die. I'm so shook up that death just doesn't seem so awful anymore, though. I'm no different from anyone else and if they're risking their lives, then so must I. But I just can't comprehend why people must die to achieve something so basic and simple as Freedom . . .

Love,

Sylvie

. . . Most of the regular SNCC workers didn't show much emotion in the open. To us it was something new, something unbelievable, that we were putting our lives on the line, that some of our team-mates had been killed; but to them it was not new. . . . I got the impression that their feelings did not differ much from those of a soldier who sees death around him. . . .

. . . You probably heard about our three workers who are presently missing in Mississippi. At first this, too, was unreal . . . but today the tension broke through . . . We had a white lawyer from Birmingham [Charles Morgan] speaking on the white Southerner. In the question period . . .

. . . a SNCC worker by the name of Jimmy Travis, who has been in the movement for years and has been shot up with a machine-gun, suddenly opened up and started to give one of the most moving statements I have ever heard . . .

. . . "It's hell in Mississippi," he repeated again and again. "We've got to change the system, to change the system!" he cried repeatedly. He talked for about a half hour, saying the same things over again, but each time it struck each of the listeners or at least me like a poison dart filling each of us with the realization of what we were getting into and the dedication needed to do it . . .

. . . After his words, everyone broke out in applause and Travis left the room in disgust. The another SNCC worker stood up and said that no one should have clapped—that Jimmy was not giving a speech. But people in the audience wanted to somehow express that they felt for and with him— and so when someone started clapping everyone joined in even though they knew that they shouldn't . . .

. . . He said what I knew all along, but it has made this place seem like a funeral parlor. People just walk around and sing, or are silent. It would be better for everyone if we just got busy and started learning techniques and policies. So far we have discussed "Why I want to go to Mississippi" for 2½ days. Damn it! I don't *want* to go; I just want to know the best way to do it . . .

What had happened in Philadelphia gave new significance to the concept of nonviolence, which was much discussed at Oxford. For some it had philosophical value; for others only a practical one.

Dear Mommy and Daddy and Toni: June 27

. . . We've been told over and over again of brutality and beating and murder. Hank says none of us really believe it inside. We probably each feel we have a lucky charm which will give us a halo of sanctity. I think we do. Part of it is the nonviolent philosophy, especially the part I now understand, which I didn't before. That is the part which teaches you to love your "enemy," how to feel true compassion for the cop who is using a cattle-prod on you, how to understand him as a human being caught in a predicament not of his own making. I think, although I'm not explaining it to you, that I now know how. When I came I thought that M. L. King and his "love your enemy" was a lot of Christian mysticism.

Now I can see it as a force and support, helping those who understand it. It makes me think that maybe I can take what is coming this summer . . .

Love,

Judy

Dear Folks:

Yesterday was non-violence day here. In the morning we heard Jim Lawson of Nashville, who gave us the word on non-violence as a way of life. Lawson speaks of a moral confrontation with one's enemies, catching the other guy's eye, speaking to him with love, if possible, and so on . . . "Violence always brings more harm to the people who use it; economic and political forces have no place in the Movement . . . etc." These are the things Lawson came up with . . . I feel very strongly that he does NOT represent the Movement.

Stokely Carmichael of SNCC rebutted him in the afternoon session: Nonviolence used to work because (1) it was new; (2) the newspapers gave it top coverage week after week, and most important (3) the demands were minor and the resistance to change was not hard-core. Now the North is tired of demonstrations, a very vigorous backlash has emerged, and the papers will only report major violence. Now we are responsible for what we do, and have to explain the stall-in instead of having it welcomed on the front pages of the press. Again most important, the movement has grown up, and is now aiming at the places where the white society really feels threatened—at jobs and at voting.

There comes a point when you get tired of being beaten and going back the next day for your beating for 5 days in a row. You get tired of being asked whether you are a Negro or a nigger, and ending up on the floor of the police station screaming at the top of your lungs that yes, you are a nigger, boss. You get tired of seeing young women smashed in the face right in front of your eyes. Stokely does not advocate violence. No SNCC workers are armed, nor are there guns in any SNCC office. What he is saying is that love and moral confrontations have no place in front of a brute who beats you till you cry nigger.

My feelings, and I think these are common, is that non-violence is a perverted way of life, but a necessary tactic and technique. It is harmful to the human person to feel that he must love a man who has a foot in his face. The *only* reason that I will not hit back is because then I will be in the hospital two weeks instead of one, and will be useless to the movement during that extra week when I can only read Gandhi's latest book on how to win friends and influence people . . .

Bill

Bayard Rustin [told how when he was] . . . in prison as a conscientious objector during the second World War, he was constantly harassed by a prison-mate, a thief, who kept throwing stones at him. One day, he went up to this man, and said, "Look friend, I'm tired of this, and so must you be. If you'd like to kill me, take this stone and bash my head in with it. Otherwise, let's stop . . ." He [added] that he hadn't been courageous, because he chose a moment when there were many people around. The man was very confused. He stood there glaring for a long, long minute, and then walked away, never to throw stones again. Now the point of this . . . the efficacy of non-violence . . . was minor to me in comparison with the impact of what he said as an indication of the kind of person I felt him to be. That is, when he said it, I actually believed the story . . .

The last night of orientation for the second group at Oxford arrived. The first bus stood waiting to leave; the volunteers traveled at night so as to arrive in Mississippi during the daytime. There was little doubt in anyone's mind that the missing three were dead.

Jim Forman of SNCC spoke, and then Bob Moses.

June 27

. . . Before the first bus pulled out last night Bob Moses, his head hanging, his voice barely audible, tried to tell us what he feels about being responsible for the creation of situations in which people get killed. His only rationales (and obviously they don't satisfy him) are that he asks no one to risk what he himself will not risk and that people were getting killed for similar reasons before Civil Rights workers became active. Looking at us sitting in the same room where the 3 missing men had been last week, Moses almost seemed to be wanting all of us to go home.

. . . He talked of the problem of good and evil . . . of a book which is one of my greatest favorites, a rather unknown book by the Englishman, J. R. R. Tolkien, *The Lord of the Ring* . . . the hero gains a means of ultimate power which he

38

does not want. Yet this power becomes a necessity to him until in the end he is unable to yield it voluntarily, and in a very great sense, he must sacrifice that which is best in himself . . . For those of us who knew the book, it was a great and beautiful moment and it gave us an understanding which we might otherwise never have had . . .

. . . He talked about how, when you spend all your times fighting evil, you become preoccupied with it and terribly weary. There may be more people killed this summer, but that won't in any way deter us from what we are trying to do. Negroes who have challenged authorities in Mississippi have always been harassed or killed and we're trying to change that, not succumb to it. We're going to do the job we have to do.

. . . Then Bob talked directly to the freedom school teachers. He begged them to be patient with their students. There's a difference between being slow and being stupid, he said. The people you will be working with aren't stupid. But they're slow, so slow.

He finished, stood for a moment, then walked out the door. Inside the auditorium there was total silence. Finally, from far in the back, a single girl's voice started to sing: "They say that freedom is a constant sorrow . . ."

. . . Slowly the voices in the room joined in. We stood with our arms around each other and we sang for each other. I stood between a boy I knew from Morehouse and a girl I knew from Carleton. And I felt the boy reach across behind me and hold the girl as well as me. I felt his love go through me, whom he knew and loved, to a girl he did not know well but whom he loved also. On the other side of this girl stood a woman who had taught at Spelman whom I knew and loved and who gave her love to this girl she did not know . . .

The group sang in one voice, each individual singing not for himself but for the group . . . As I sang and I felt the love of the group I realized that I loved all equally and that the difference was that I knew some better than others. And I knew better than ever before why I was going to Mississippi and what I am fighting for. It is for freedom—the freedom to love. It is something that none can have until everybody has it. Freedom to love all people equally and unselfishly, freedom to be a man with integrity so that there is no need to try to take others' integrity from them . . .

. . . As we sang, we all must have thought of our three
39

who already died this summer in Mississippi. Everyone cried; either inside or out. We sang more, all kinds of songs, but the mood remained sad—sad because we have to do what we have to do, but not pity . . .

June 26

. . . Must write—thoughts are going crazy. Bob Moses just told us now is the time to back out. Should I? I don't know—I am scared shitless. I don't want to go to Mississippi. Why? Is it because I am scared or because the program isn't for me? No, program is good—people are dedicated—means of project conform with the end says Mario. Civil Rights Bill won't help—people are being killed—got to help. Pray. Forman says much of the tension will leave when we reach Mississippi. Father Keating says stick it out, give project a chance. Perhaps I should only write down optimistic things to reduce dissonance but I must be honest. Little Negro kid said I would be killed in Mississippi and not to go if they weren't paying me. He's too glib. Nevertheless, he really shook me up. Damon isn't going. Wish I knew why. I have no one to turn to but me—and God. Perhaps He will give me a sign—Iwo Jima—cat who raised the flag is still living. But I ask for too many signs. Tomorrow I am leaving.

Before you all came, Mississippi was white man's land.
Now it will become human land.

Freedom School pupil
Greenwood, Mississippi

2 / At Home in a Black World

Now it is one o'clock and our bus is traveling down a Tennessee road, far into the country. I have always thought that between the hours of one and three A.M. America comes closest to realizing her promise. There is a unity among all her travelers . . . We all inhabit the same night in the same land. But somehow that is not enough.

The entry of the volunteers into Mississippi—mostly by bus and singing together on the way—was very different from the first lonely trip made there by Bob Moses four years earlier. Mississippi was almost virgin territory then. Civil rights workers hadn't even tried to enter the state until 1952; the first "agitator" was shot and killed, the second was shot and run out of the state. Moses' foray turned out to be the seed of the Mississippi Summer Project. Between August, 1961, and the fall of 1963, voter registration workers—mainly from the Student Nonviolent Coordinating Committee—spread into several parts of the state. That November, a Freedom Vote took place in which 80,000 disenfranchised Negroes cast their ballots for their own candidates in a mock state election which demonstrated that they would vote if they could. Students from Yale and Stanford came down to work on the Freedom Vote, thus extending civil rights work into seven more counties and establishing a successful precedent for the 1964 volunteers.

The needs of the Mississippi Negro clearly called for a campaign which could be waged only with the help of a lot of outsiders and a lot of outside money. After a long winter and spring of anaylsis, debate, recruitment, confusion and scrambling for funds, the Summer Project of 1964 finally began. Over 1,000 people entered the state of Mississippi. There was, first, the core group of 650 volunteers from 37 states (with a sprinkling from England, New Zealand and Australia) who are represented in this book. Then came the hundreds of ministers, doctors, nurses, lawyers and performing artists, to lend their abilities for two weeks or longer. Of the entire band, a very large majority were white people from outside the South, not so much because they were chosen that way as because more whites than Negroes applied and were financially able to come (every volunteer was supposed to bring $150 for his stay in Mississippi plus guaranteed bail money).

The mechanics of the project's administration bewildered more than a few observers. Nominally, it was run by COFO —the Council of Federated Organizations—a Mississippi-based union of local groups, SNCC, CORE, King's Southern Christian Leadership Conference, and the Mississippi State Conference of NAACP branches (not the national NAACP). COFO had administered the Freedom Vote of 1963.

In actuality, SNCC and CORE did almost the entire job. Mississippi's five Congressional districts were divided between those two organizations, with SNCC staffing and financing the work in four of them. Of the 100 staff members on the Summer Project, 76 were from SNCC. Robert Moses of SNCC was the director of the project and Program Director for COFO; Dave Dennis from CORE held the post of Assistant Program Director; Dr. Aaron Henry, state President of the NAACP and a longtime resident, served as President of COFO. Headquarters for the project was a hectic office in the Negro neighborhood of Jackson, with almost as many telephones as people and 1017 Lynch Street for its address. Up in the town of Greenwood, about a two hour drive away, SNCC established its national headquarters for the summer. Nobody was quite ready for action when the first wave of volunteers hit.

Dear friends,   Ruleville, Miss.

Last Saturday four of us took the long ride from Oxford to Memphis in a small Corvette which was rigged with a mike so that a CBS sound car behind us could record our profound thoughts as we went into battle. . . . We were all too tired to be the least bit profound. I felt quite relaxed during most of the 14 hour drive. Mississippi seemed very remote! At midnite we pulled up to a Howard Johnson's Motel just a few miles from the border. The CBS crew went through great contortions in arranging rooms for us all which could be written off on their expense account. An old man who was in the office asked us what CBS was doing. We told him. He asked why we wanted to stir up trouble. Why didn't we take care of Harlem. People in Mississippi could take care of their own problems. We were too tired to answer, but the feeling that we were in enemy territory swept in on me.

Sunday morning after the dead sleep of exhaustion I awoke with fear gripping my gut. I had a hard time forcing down breakfast. At 10 A.M. we left for the most direct route to Ruleville. When we got to the state line the camera car told us to stop at the side of the road while they went to set up a shot at the big sign that welcomes motorists to the Magnolia State. Waiting there as cars streamed past with their occupants craning their necks to look at us, we got quite spooked. We finally got the go-ahead but then had to go back past the sign for a second run. All this time we noticed a big yellow car pass back and forth. We were quite angry at the newsmen's lack of planning and precautions.

After the first ten miles across the sun-bathed delta, the acute tension started to give way to a loose-limbed anxiety. Instead of being braced for what might come, I was ready to give with it. But the fear still clutched at the back of my neck as a car full of white men approached. . . . At one point the photographer was shooting us from the back of his car ahead when a car full of white rowdies passed us on the left and observed the whole thing. Well, we made it to Ruleville and Mrs. Fannie Lou Hamer's house where some of the volunteers plus a whole lot of press and some local people were gathered. Oh, were they a welcome sight!

Love,

Mike

Moss Point, June 30

I arrived by bus with the two other girls in Moss Point yesterday afternoon. After we waited a few minutes and nobody met us, we made a call to a number we'd been given and were told a ride was coming. We were then approached by a big heavy double-chinned drawling Southern stereotype, who turned out to be the chief deputy sheriff, one "Caesar" Byrd. He claimed he was looking for "a bunch of runaway girls from the North" and had us hand over our identification. After some prolonged verbal fencing which went something like this . . . "What part of town you staying in?" "With some friends." etc., it became clear that he knew damn well who we were and we knew that he knew when he finally gave up the circumlocution with, "You come straight down from Oxford?"

I must confess I was scared silly at first, and was already fumbling in my pocket to make sure I had a dime for my one call from jail, but actually it's just as well it happened—he'd find out about us anyway . . .

Shortly after this little interview, a car picked us up, and a fat laughing Negro woman drove us to our destination. Sheriff Byrd followed us in his car most of the way. The police drove past the COFO office six times in half an hour tonight, and this afternoon a car full of whites stopped and took down all the license numbers of cars in front of the office. But we got theirs, too, even-stephen. . . .

Sunday saw the arrival of about 25 Freedom School teachers in Canton. They came in on the train about noon and we had six or seven cars there to meet them. . . . A couple of carloads of cops pulled up suddenly and stood around while we unloaded all the suitcases and equipment and put them in the cars. . . . The county Sheriff and the chief of police asked us to go down to the police station to register. We decided we would cooperate so that our lack of cooperation couldn't be held against us in case of trouble. [This was not COFO policy, which generally advised against agreeing to register.] We were all registered, giving our names, home addresses, local addresses, intentions, ages, and various other identifying details. We also had our pictures taken with a little blackboard with our name written on it hanging around our necks. Then we were issued cards which signified that we had been duly registered with the Canton police department.

As a part of the show at the police station we were asked to listen to a tape which had been prepared by the attorneys of the city of Canton. . . . We were told that the girls might be raped by the very Negroes whom we have come to help and that the men might be stabbed or worse by the same people. The tape [said] that our presence here is very much resented by the white citizens and that they would be extremely happy if we were to change our minds and go home. We were told that we are uninvited guests in the county—which remark was challenged by one of the workers who reminded the chief of police that we had been invited by the Negro citizens of the county, if not by the whites. This would seem to constitute a rather good invitation as the county is 72% Negro. . . .

But usually the whites just stared—sullen or curious or hateful—and the volunteers found their fear receding.

. . . We were really expecting much worse. Most of us

would not have been too surprised if everybody had been arrested as we crossed the Miss. border and/or beaten. The disappearance of the three boys, tragic as it is, is mild compared to what we expected.

Their new homes were with Negro families or on Negro college campuses, but always in a Negro community. Some of the families had their own farms, some had no security at all.

Dear Anne,   Itta Bena, June 28

It's a hot lazy Sunday afternoon. I want to try to give you a description of Itta Bena and the place where we're staying.

The Negro neighborhood is literally "on the other side of the railroad tracks." To get over to the white and downtown area you have to either walk past several warehouses, small factories, etc., or cross the railroad tracks. The Negro neighborhood hasn't got a single paved street in it. It's all dirt and gravel roads. The houses vary from really beat-up shacks to fairly good looking cottages. The beat-up places predominate. There are lots of smelly outhouses and many of the houses have no inside water.

During the day it seems as if there is nothing but small children, hordes of them, and old people sitting on porches. There are quite a few churches. These have the most uncomfortable benches imaginable. I really can't do a good job of describing it; but then I don't have to—you've seen places like this town in movies and magazines a hundred times. But to see the place in the real is so different from seeing pictures of it. It's really there—you feel the heat, breathe the dust, smell the outhouses, hear the kids and the chickens.

John and I are staying with a 67-year-old woman named Rosa Lee Williams. She owns her place, so she doesn't have to worry about being thrown out.

Her house is on East Freedom Street. The street runs along the RR tracks. Across the street is a row of corn and then the RR tracks and a cotton field beyond. The house has a living room, with a double bed that John and I sleep in, a bedroom where Mrs. Williams sleeps and where we eat, then a small kitchen. The only running water in the place is in the toilet. No sinks are hooked up, so we wash out of buckets etc., but at least we have a flush toilet. Those outhouses are too much!

Mrs. Williams gets $4.00 a week from each of us for room. Originally she said she wasn't going to cook for us, but she's

45

always doing it anyhow, so we're giving her another $4.00 a week. She said she didn't want the extra money, but she's on a pension and welfare, so she probably needs the money. She's really gotten crazy about us. She calls us 'Lil' Bro' " and "Big Bro' " (Bro' is brother). She had a broken leg which wasn't set quite right, so she sort of limps. She also has an improperly set collarbone; it was broken when she was fighting with someone over a shotgun. She's still mad at the Deputy Sheriff for not giving her back the shotgun.

There's an old preacher, Mr. Bevel, two doors down. Another preacher in Itta Bena decided that it would be better for John and me to move in with him because he has a phone. When we mentioned it to Mrs. Williams, she was furious with Bevel for trying to take us away and we had to stop talking about it for fear she'd start a fight with him.

She's really a fiery and fast moving old woman. The first night we were here, Willie, John and I moved the bed into the living room. She was in the bedroom about 3 seconds before us and had the bed half apart before we were in the room. While we were setting it up in the living room she was running around mopping under where we were putting the bed. Before we went to sleep she brought in a can and put it under the bed. She said it was for "spittin" (she chews tobacco).

She keeps as clean a house as is possible with all the dust from the road blowing in. She's meticulous about flies and mosquitos and usually sprays the place at night.

She's sort of a lonely old woman and I guess she enjoys having people around the house. She said that the last of her children died after the influenza epidemic of 1918. Her husband was a preacher and she's a retired midwife.

John and I both started having diarrhea last night. Must be due to new bugs in the water, food, etc. It should be over in a few days.

I love you,
Roy

Greetings Ed, from the Delta—   Tchula, July 6

My views on ruralfucking America are well known. Yet here I am living on a farm for the first time in my life—and enjoying it . . . The Negroes here are independent farmers and live in small wooden houses with no running water and no sanitation facilities but they generally have a TV set, a freezer, a truck and a tractor—luxury that few sharecroppers or casual workers in Mississippi can hope to attain.

In the two bedroom house in which I live we have 5 small girls, a baby, 3 teenage girls, and the mother and father, one 11-year old boy and a grandmother, plus the two of us volunteers. The five children sleep in pinwheel fashion in one bed. Cephas (the other volunteer—a Negro) and I share a room all to ourselves. The house is kept immaculately by the three girls. Many Northern women could take lessons from them. The food is unbelievable, the proverbial farmhand's meal with biscuits, eggs, rice, cornbread, sausage for breakfast and so much dinner that no three people could eat it . . .

Best,
Mike

. . . Shaw is a small town (1.500), sharply divided into Negro and white sections . . . I stay with five other girls in a house of ten people, two dogs, a cat and an assortment of several thousand bugs. An ants' nest was in my bed the first night, a bees' nest in the kitchen, a wasps' nest in the bedroom . . . Two of the girls left within a week . . .

Hattiesburg, July 4

I am spoiled here in a solid, middle-class type home, and feel guilty about not sharing the more primitive living conditions of many other volunteers. Living with so many people —there are 16 here—has been surprisingly easy, but I got some insight into what it would be like without plumbing the other day. I had the misfortune of waking up with an urgent need to urinate. Of course there is only one bathroom, and the man of the house was in the tub. I paced the floor as long as I could and finally ran for Mrs. ——. She got the pot, and I took it into the bedroom. Now my room-mate was still asleep, and she is a terror in the morning. You can't imagine how terrified I was of her wrath and my humiliation as I squatted above the ringing tin! . . .

Love,
Susan

Mileston, June 30

Man, like I don't even believe what I just did. You really had to be here to appreciate it. I took a bath. But no ordinary bath 'cause there's no running water. No, we take this bucket out in the back yard and fill it with water warmed over a fire. It's pitch black so we shine Mr. Clark's truck lights on the bucket. Then I strip down naked and stand in the bucket and wash. That is the way you take a bath around here.

But the most significant new experience for the white volunteers was their reception by the Negro community.

Dear people,

Batesville welcomed us triumphantly—at least Black Batesville did. Children and adults waved from their porches and shouted hello as we walked along the labyrinth of dirt paths and small wooden houses that characterize the Negro section of any Southern town. In a few days scores of children knew us and called to us by name. We had been warned to expect fear and hostility, but we were immediately invited to live and eat in Negro homes and to speak in Negro churches. For many local citizens our coming was a religious event; I found it difficult to be cynical. Sometimes when we pass by, the children cheer. . . .

Geoff

Gulfport

. . . Fifty times a day people come up to us and thank us and tell us what we're doing is so fine, so good. The kids, playing with boards in the dust, have the greatest smiles. When we're out going from door to door to get people to register, we see a kid get up and run inside. "There they is" we hear. We are "they" and everyone knows who "they" is.

Greenville

It's amazing how you can grow to almost love a place so quickly. The Negro community has been so receptive and welcoming. The other night, a woman who has 17 children invited 20 of us over for dinner. It was a good dinner, too.

Canton, July 10

We are constantly on display when we're at the house; neighbors file in and out to have a look at us. The older ladies like to feel our skin; the kids are fascinated by our hair; everybody makes an appraisal of some sort—either we're "skinny" or "pretty" or "clean" or "young." When we go walking with [the two] widows [we're staying with,] one of them invariably greets each passerby with "have you seen my girls yet?"

There are the old men and women in old clothing whom you know have little money and none to spare, who stop you as you are leaving the church after addressing the congregation and press a dollar into your hand and say, "I've waited 80 years for you to come and I just have to give you this little bit to let you all know how much we appreciate your coming. I prays for your safety every night, son. God bless you all." And then they move down the stone steps and disappear along the red clay road lined with tall green trees and houses tumbling down.

Gulfport

Time and time again when we go into a restaurant or bar, we start to pay, only to be told that the bill has been taken care of. People bring over a dozen eggs or cake or invite us to dinner. The hospitality seems like that of the old frontier, with its house raisings and quilting bees.

Hattiesburg

Sometimes I think that all the decency the Mississippi human contains is encased in black walls. They're slow and talkative, but they'd shake hands with a mule if it came up to speak to them; if they had one cigarette left, they'd offer to halve it with you before they'd smoke it in front of your face. All this from people to whom $20 is a fortune . . .

And a medical student assigned to Meridian wrote:

I gave "medical" advice earlier this week to a father, whose son had an abscess on his chest. I told them to take the kids to a doctor. The father thanked me and kissed my hand. I was embarrassed and didn't know what to do, so I kissed his hand.

Sometimes, during the first days of the project, the local men showed their concern by standing guard—unasked—at offices and homes where the volunteers were staying. Once in a while the offers of protection created awkward situations. . . .

Gulfport, July 25

We had a problem with a man, and some of his friends, who took it upon himself to protect us from the white men who visited us yesterday. He came over at night with his friends and brought along a machine gun and ammunition. And told us not to worry. But he finally got ticked off at us, because we got ticked off at him. That machine-gun made us edgy. . . .

But as the volunteers lived longer in Mississippi, the guns seemed more understandable. They learned on the spot— from the things that befell their own hosts and hostesses.

Dear John and Cleo,   Canton, July 10

Our hostesses are brave women. And their fear is not at all mixed with resentment of us, but that makes it none the easier for them. The other morning a local newscaster said that someone was reported to have offered someone else $400 to bomb all the houses where volunteers are staying. I'm not convinced that that particular story has any basis, but it touched off the terror that must lie latent always in our sisters' hearts. I overheard one of them on the telephone: "My guhls probly think I'm out of mah head; I been singin' all mornin, every song I knows—I just has to." And she had been, moaning "Lord have musee" in between the songs. I talked with her a little bit. She told me she knows people have suffered and died too long and that we must take risks now so it won't go on forever. But that doesn't make the risk any less painful to bear. She sleeps with a hatchet under her bed. She told me she used to have a gun under her pillow until one night when she almost accidentally shot a neighbor boy. . . .

Jo

Shaw, July

The Negroes here have been pretty courageous, taking us into their homes and churches. Many of the homes we are staying in were shot up when the people went down to register during the past two years. One family got scared and ask two of us to leave after a car parked all night in front of their home a couple of nights ago—imagine having somebody sit in front of your home all night. Another person was fired from his job yesterday because two of us were staying with him.

Ruleville, July

. . . we have been given a wonderfully warm welcome

wherever we have gone. In Ruleville the mayor had spent a week warning the Negroes that we were coming to kill them. (The mayor was told by one of the local Negro ministers, "You're so low you're going to need a step ladder to climb into Hell.") Yet we were given the best of everything, and housing was found for all forty of us. Two people have already lost their jobs for housing us, and yet in each case half a dozen families begged us to stay with them after we had had to leave. . . .

More and more, the volunteers found that the people they had come to help were helping them; those whom they had come to teach grammar and history were giving them lessons in life and love.

Dear Mom and Dad,   Gulfport, July 4

. . . You both know how critical I always have been of other people—always expecting a high level of performance and rather arrogant when the level is not reached. Thus I was a little worried, coming down here, where—because of a completely different cultural environment—people couldn't possibly meet those standards, or even aim toward them. That is, I was worried that I would tend to be extremely critical of the people around me, even though intellectually I knew how ridiculous it was.

But this has not occurred. . . . When I talk to someone while I am canvassing, I am able to accept them completely as they are. . . . If Mrs. X can read, fine; if not, I can enjoy talking to her about her life and experiences. Perhaps I've been finding that people everywhere have more in common that I once thought: humanity is so much more basic than education or intellectual achievement.

Related to this—I have met some of the most amazing, great people. Out of nowhere, seemingly, come little old women with so much warmth and wisdom that I almost cry. There's little Mrs. Rachel Fairley, who is about 65 and wonderful and crisp and brisk, yet full of God and sympathy. She's always praying for me—and for the three lost near Philadelphia. . . .

Yesterday, around 7 P.M. I marched up on the steps of a dark little falling apart house. Mrs. Brotherns—the lady of the house, I later learned—invited me in. (I keep being invited in for "some barbecue or a cold drink or a rest on the front porch.") Her husband was a beautiful man of about 59, great masses of graying hair. He was crippled with arthritis and thus could not write and could not read either.

It began to rain. We sat in a small dark room, lighted only by a brief flame in the fireplace where Mrs. Brotherns was cooking dinner. Their three adopted children sat on the floor and read from school books or counted bottletops, while the two old people looked on with love. The whole scene was from another century—especially because the little boy had a self-made bow and arrow, bent from a stick and tied with some cord. He proudly shot an arrow into the bushes across the street as I watched. . . .

Love,
Ellen

Meridian, Aug. 11

This is a very front porch community. People seem to know all the details of their neighbors' lives but there is very little judgment. This is not a puritanical society. Pity is somehow blended with complete acceptance of sensuality, sexuality, except if it's interracial—a white girl taking to a Negro boy is terrifying to them and with reason . . . By sensuality I guess I mean what Baldwin meant—a way of being *present* in everything they do.

Tchula, August 30

There is some strong ambivalence which goes with this work. I sometimes fear that I am only helping to integrate some beautiful people into modern white society with all of its depersonalization (I suppose that has something to do with its industrial nature). It isn't 19th century pastoral romanticism which I feel, but a genuine respect and admiration for a culture which, for all the trouble, still isn't as commercialized and depersonalized as is our Northern mass culture. It is somewhat annoying to see a grubby little Negro cafe with a four foot by six foot tall full color picture of a young handsome Negro in a white dinner jacket next to his beautiful young Negro wife in a $200 cocktail dress in the backyard of their $40,000 brick home standing in front of a massive barbecue with prime ribs of beef and tender young duckling in beautiful glistening copperware serving Pabst Blue Ribbon Beer. A typical American Negro couple on a typical Sunday afternoon. Let's all escape and be like the white man . . .

Dear Mom,   Holmes County, July 8

I have become so close to the family I am staying with—eleven people—that Mrs. H. finally paid me a great compliment. She was introducing me to one of her Negro women friends and said, "This is Nancy, my adopted daughter!" I baby-sat for her one night and in general we have become very close friends. She is a beautiful mother. My favorite picture of her is sitting peacefully in a summer chair with her 2-year old baby girl in her lap; the baby, sucking her bottle, with one hand inside her mother's dress resting on her bosom. It is such a human sight; such love oozes from this house I can't begin to explain. All evening I have little children crawling over me and big boys, 16, my buddies, combing my hair, confiding in me, appreciating me, because I will open my heart and mind to them and listen and care for them and show my concern. I may be sex- and love-starved, as some like to picture me, but at least I have faced the problem and have found my own inner peace by being with people who have not forgotten how to love.

Really, to tell you the honest truth, I am just a little bit tired of hearing you and others, and for a long time even myself, think, worry, discuss, write and talk about all the deep down psychological reasons for your personal problems. When I see these simple people living lives of relative inner peace, love, honor, courage and humor, I lose patience with people who sit and ponder their belly buttons. . . .

Love,
Nancy

The happiness of the white volunteer sometimes suggested a feeling of assuaged guilt: "these people who should reject me for what my race has done to them are not full of hatred but warm acceptance." It was a surprise, and a relief, . . .

Hattiesburg, July 8

I am not yet sure that I know why Southern Negroes seem to be less suspicious of our intentions than would Harlem Negroes for instance, but I definitely believe it is there.

Vicksburg

One day when I was canvassing I met Mr. Brown. I told him my name is Ann. He said yes, Miss Ann, pleased to meet you. He is a young Negro teacher in the all-Negro Temple High School and of course he had no contact with white people before, except as Mr., Mrs., "Massa",—well, I said please call me Ann—and Ran, there was nothing so beautiful as the rest of the conversation. At every opportunity he had, he said Ann—he didn't just say Ann—he rolled the name around his tongue, savored the taste and sang it, listening to the echo in the back of his mind. He played with the word as a child would play with a new and fascinating toy, as a person would delight in the ecstasy of a new-found love. And that conversation has left a mark on me. I hear the name—a loved word—the start of something so big, so beautiful, so new. . . .

Ran, this is something really big—yes, a revolution—a New Way of Living and Being. It's so different from the North where there is the intense, bitter hatred which makes working in Harlem or Roxbury or Philadelphia so heartbreaking because there is this invisible wall. Here there is Fear (I am referring now to the Negroes altho the whites are included) and when you reach that fear and stop it—as you can with some of the college and high school-age kids—there is a clear path—and this is where that great Change will come. . . . There is hope here that does not exist in the North . . .

One of the several reasons for this hope seemed to be religion. Nothing made a deeper impression on the volunteers than the black Mississippian's sense of God.

Hi again,   Flora, July 13

. . . Jim and I have moved in with a little man who looks like Mr. Magoo and who bakes wonderful bread. He must be 75 years old, but he's tough, still working, and willing to undergo danger. He spends nearly all his spare time in reading the Bible, and like many of the people here, he takes its teachings to heart. The faith of these people here is amazing and not a dead form, like in most Northern churches. The services are lively, and it seems like the people follow the theory of Love Thy Enemy better than any people I've come in contact with. They have every reason to hate the white man, but I think they really don't. . . .

Doug

Holly Springs, July 6

. . . Sunday I went to a real whoop and holler church, with people shouting, screaming and stomping. The sermon began as a talk and ended as a song. The preacher jumped up and down and had tears running down his face. He finally was overcome by the sheer power of his word and started to sing 'This Little Light of Mine' in the middle of a sentence. We joined him, and people came up to grab his hands. I was one of them. This was the only House of God I had ever run into in my life. Amen! It was real, powerful and glorious.

Vicksburg

I went to Church today, the third time since I've been here . . . It's just like the scene in *Go Tell it on The Mountain*—but it's real—there's a direct tie between every person in that church and God, and every person with me and I with them.

Tonight was different from the first time . . . I left the church, wondering the eternal question of God, which we so easily answer with terms of science and evolution and theories of the Beginning . . . I cannot say God, I cannot think God, yet I cannot so easily dismiss the thought of some higher order of things—and after so long I cannot accept it and I want to run to some Wise One and plead "Tell me, tell me—what is the answer?" And there is no Wise One to answer me— and now I shall never know and I am afraid to read again what I am writing to you now with such speed because I know two weeks later, I will say to you—well, I was very tired when I wrote this to you and I will forget how I felt and I will sink back into that middle class existence you and I and our clan live in. No—I do not mean that exactly, for we do think and really wonder and worry and hope and weep and feel—but it's sort of a rut. For we think more or less in the context in which we were brought up— Aye, liberal and thought-provoking though it is, it is still enslaving us. . . .

Moss Point, July 8

. . . On Sunday I heard a very fine preacher in a little ramshackle church down the road. A congregation of about twelve adults and a few children, scattered around to look like more, in flowered hats, little girls in bright pink dresses, sat listening and most fanning themselves with stiff cardboard fans which said "Friendly Funeral Home" on the back. This one gesture I would pick to show a big piece of Mississippi life; this slow fanning in the heat, the head cocked sideways, eyes half-closed, lazy, feeling the wind on wet skin. . . .

The preacher was a visiting bishop, a great orator, almost a black nationalist, shouting out about Africa . . . no Uncle Tom he, and Pharaoh he said was "not a man, but the symbol of a government, a system, like Uncle Sam, the man with the long beard, always there even if the President gets shot." He spoke like this, loudly and earnestly, to the little fanning congregation, which answered now and then with a quiet "oyeslord" and "ain't it the truth" to the rhythm of their fanning.

Ruleville

At the service this morning, in the interminable prayer of thanksgiving, I was ready to gag. These people—who for sincerity and simplicity of belief are unrivalled by ten times as many Central Churches—have no reward for their faith. I wanted to tell them, but of course I won't, because it's all they have, and I admire them for it . . .

Dear Mom,   Hattiesburg, 3:30 A.M.

. . . I really can't understand role of God and 'His will be done.' I think we should stop mouthing that cliche and start looking at vast sickness and decay in organized religion. Outside of the National Council of Churches which breathes a little fresh air (some of the ministers are really sharp)* and men like Mallette, Clemens, and Sheehan, religion bugs me so . . . Been reading that 'liberal' encyclical. Not very impressed. Also, big news from Jackson: Bishop of Mississippi declares all first grades [in parochial schools] should be opened on non-racial basis. Too bad most schools just happen to have their quotas filled up already. Bless our monsignor. He thinks with such foresight. Yea, social justice!

Love,
Dick

It was difficult to talk about Negro faith without coming back to the facts of Negro life. The first gift of black Mississippi to the white volunteers had been a sense of human beauty; the second was an education in some aspects of America which most of them had never confronted before.

Ruleville

There are people here without food and clothing. Kids that eat a bit of bread for breakfast, chicken necks for dinner. Kids that don't have clothes to go to school in. Old, old people, and young people chop [hoe] cotton from sun up till sun down for $3 a day. They come home exhausted, it's not

*The NCC sent ministers for consultation by the volunteers when needed.

enough to feed their family on. It's gone before they earn it. . . . Some people down here get welfare. It amounts to about $45 a month. Pay the average $15 rent and you have a family "living" on $30 for four weeks. . . .

In Sunflower County alone there are 4,270 Negro families and 720 white families living in poverty. At the same time there are just over 100 families who own and control most of the county. Negro people are being kicked out of jobs, off sharecropping etc. to remove them from Mississippi. Mechanization of farms (plantations), usage of agricultural sprays, etc. provide the excuse and the agency to force the Negro to leave Mississippi. By no means is this the only means used, though . . . Mississippi might be described as a state where people are harassed and intimidated—once because they were black and the means of production; now because they are black and a challenge to the status quo.

The other day a shipment of food and clothing arrived for the Negroes. Man, you don't know the "trouble" that something like this makes. The needs down here have to be measured by the truck loads or train loads. The shipment does not bring enough to go around. . . .

Tchula, July 16

One lady I talked to last Saturday makes $2.50 a day working 7 days a week from 7 A.M. to 10 P.M. as cook and maid in a white home. She is old and alone and afraid to do anything for fear she will lose her only income and with it the tiny wooden house she saved for through many years of chopping and picking cotton. She never drinks a coke but fixes instead a penny Kool-aid on a hot day, to save the 9 cents she needs for her house and bills.

Dear Mom, Dad and Shari,   Mileston, July 23

We've been learning a little about conditions on some local plantations.

One plantation worker secretly left the plantation to come and ask us for help. He gets up at 3:30 A.M. and works on a tractor until dusk—for $5 a day, six days a week. His wife picks cotton for $2.50 a day. Two years ago he borrowed $250 from his plantation owner; since then, his "owner" has taken $10 a week out of his pay and hasn't stopped. A year and a half ago, when the debt had been paid, he asked the "owner" how much he still owed, he was told $100, and got the same answer ten weeks later (with the $10 a week still being deducted). He asked once too often, because the next week, after his boss discovered that he attended citizenship

57

classes, the boss came to him with a note saying he owed $650. His boss and a local deputy sheriff are co-owners of the plantation . . .

Love,

Joel

Dear Mom and Dad,   Shaw, July 4

One day has passed in Shaw and the other America is opening itself before my naive, middle-class eyes. The cockroaches draw patterns across the floor and table and make a live patchwork on the bed. Sweat covers my skin and cakes brown in my joints—wrist, elbow, knee, neck. Mosquito bites, red specks on white background.

The four-year old grandson is standing by my side. I wonder how our presence now will effect him when he is a man?

I saw other children today who bore the marks of the Negro in rural Mississippi. One had a protruding navel the size of the stone he held in his hand. Several had distended stomachs.

Is America really the land that greets its visitors with "Send me your tired, your poor, your helpless masses to breathe free . . ."?

There is no Golden Door in Shaw.

Every statistic stood now for things the volunteers had seen with their own eyes, for people they lived with, people who fed them and protected them.

Hattiesburg, July 4

Every time I talk to people, I hear about things which bring tears to my eyes. I have begun, finally, to feel deep inside me this horrible double existence Negroes have to lead in both North and South . . . the strategies they must learn to survive without either going crazy or being physically maimed—or destroyed. Mr. Reese describes how a Negro must learn to walk through a crowd: weaving, slightly hunched—shuffling helps—in order to be as humbly inconspicuous as possible. . . . Then I hear from men who served in Korea or elsewhere, that they alone had no flag to fight for . . . I talked with a fellow whose closest buddy [in the Army] had been a white man from Mississippi; when they were homeward bound on the train and they crossed the Mason-Dixon line, the white man left his seat beside the Negro to change seats with another Negro.

I could go on and on about all the people I've met . . .

Baby, it takes coming down here to grasp all this, no matter how many books we've read.

Ruleville, July

Most of us . . . are from schools and families where sensitivity to pain is a very important virtue. I have made here the discovery that sensitivity is one of those virtues that depends upon the certainty of food and roof. . . . Here, one who is sensitive to pain will soon be reduced to a mass of wounds and hurts. . . .

Dear Stark,   Meridian, June 30

. . . About the three missing men: there have been so many things like this that have never made any difference because no one has heard of them. Like the Negro [Herbert Lee] who was shot on the front lawn of the Liberty courthouse three years ago by a member of the state legislature. A Negro witness [Louis Allen] testified that it was self-defense, because of course he was scared. Then in January for some reason the sheriff or someone beat him up and broke his jaw. So he called up the FBI and told them he'd lied before, but the FBI wouldn't protect him and he was killed within 24 hours. Maybe you've heard this, most people haven't. But of course he was a Mississippi Negro. . . .

Love,
Edna

There are almost no sidewalks in the Negro neighborhoods. The red clay dirt is hard and the sun won't quit . . . The poverty and sorrow of the neighborhoods doesn't leave you. I've been to hundreds of houses I could kick down with my feet and a small hammer. And I've seen the hands of these people, swollen and bruised, hard and calloused from years of work at practically no pay and whatever the pay was, it was always half what a white man would get for the same job. And I realized very suddenly and forcefully that these are my people and their sorrow is mine also. And since we are of this country our grief is collective whether the rest of the country admits it or not . . .

What had happened, in a very short time, was that the Negro's world had become the volunteer's world, while the white world—in most cases, their own—had become an alien, frightening and ugly place.

I really cannot describe how sick I think this state is. I really cannot tell you how repulsed I am by this state, nor how fervently I think something has to be done down here. I cannot describe the fears, the tensions and the uncertainties of living here. When I walk, I am always looking at cars and people: if Negro, they are my friends; if white, I am frightened and walk faster. When driving and a car approaches, I am always asking: black? white?

Laurel

We feel safe here surrounded by the Negro community. The feeling of security evaporates when we go downtown . . . They all look like Snopes family to me. . . .

Meridian, mid-summer

We live so completely within the Negro community that there is little confrontation of the white community. I noticed the other day that some white kids I passed looked to me as though they'd been washed too hard.

Dear people,   Batesville, July 26

Coming down from Crenshaw yesterday evening, I was in Reverend John's station wagon (with Jersey tags). We stopped in Batesville for gas at a white station, and two Negro workers there moved over to work on the car while the white proprietor collected the money from the Reverend. The young fellow (younger than I) who started cleaning the windshield kept giving me a beautifully friendly half-smile as he wiped the glass, a smile that seemed to be keeping a secret from the white proprietor. Every time he caught my eye, he smiled, and I was laughing back; it was wonderful communication. I said yes, please. As he bent under the hood to check the oil, I got out of the car and stood next to him as if mentioning something about the innards of the car. I asked him quietly (while the white man stood a ways away) if he smiled that way for all his white customers, or just for civil rights workers. We communicated in a stifled laugh for a minute; then he answered, "Just civil rights." It's getting harder and harder for me to listen with a straight face when a cracker tells me that "our niggers don't want you here."

Love,
Jim

But this new identity wasn't always so simple . . .

Before coming to Mississippi, we had been told that whites considered all civil rights workers not only "nigger lovers" but white Negroes as well. We had also been told that in the colored community you may soon be considered black.

But a white man never turns black in Mississippi. Sometimes you feel you've crossed the color line when a woman tells you about her fears and tells how she lies to the white folks but secretly hates them. She has probably never talked like this to a white man before; for a moment you believe you are turning black. Yet there are still the long silences and the incomprehensible phrases. Women still call me Mr. Geoff instead of Geoff, and old men offer their chairs. That doesn't disappear when they start to talk about their fear. And neither does your secret belief—which the old men and women encourage—that you are, after all, superior. Maybe this will all change when you've been here longer and when you visit a family for the fifth time. Maybe; but you're still college educated, still play acting, and still white . . . You're still amused when in sorting out books for the Freedom library one Negro worker insists on discarding *Black Beauty* and a young local dark girl parades about with her recently discovered copy of *Pride and Prejudice*. It helps only slightly when you watch one of your fellow white volunteers throw away a copy of *Nigger of the Narcissus*. Following a marvelous dinner at the house of your local landlord, you hear yourself say "*Boy*, was that a great dinner" and you choke involuntarily on the expletive. You can't forget that you're still white . . .

I am staying with one other project worker at the home of an elderly midwife widow. Last night we met two of her neighbors and spoke a limited amount with others young and old. . . . I felt that at any moment they would be willing to say "Ma'am" to me if I should raise my voice. How can I help create an honest relationship after years of lies, of words that came from the lips and not the heart?

When the men from town here are drunk, they come up to the house saying "shit, I'm not scared of anything, hear." By the next day they are crawling again. The fear in their faces is pathetic. Last night a drunk man latched on to us. He kept talking about two things: he fought hard in Korea (shell shock and two lost toes, he has) and when he returned, the same people he was fighting for treated him like a dog; his wife died three months before. He took us to see his home ("it's open to you anytime"). There were three people there, his child, his mother-in-law, and her husband. The adults were all staggering drunk. There's not much recreation for Negroes except drinking and screwing, empty as life can be. The father-in-law was drunk but he was still *terrified*. You should see the faces, the eyes, of the men who are broken. The mother-in-law started talking: "sit down god-darned it, I want to talk to you. The white people treat us colored folk so *bad*. There's nothing we can do. They killed those three boys, they'll kill us all. What can we do?" I wish I could remember what all she said. She was so drunk she didn't "Yasuh" us and she swore at us. That was good, because she told the truth (what she really felt) and for a white man to get this from a Mississippi Negro is exceptional . . .

Some of the proud Negroes among us say we are trying to save the black man's body and the white man's soul. But we have to save both souls. Many of these people are so smashed and whiplashed by the treatment they've gotten, that they're lost . . . This is the worst thing about segregation, it breaks people, it makes boys ("hey, boy, come here") out of men. The men are often so pitifully weak—unable to decide anything or to do anything. Another problem is that when the people get stronger, they often release against whites all the anger which they've repressed . . .

We are frustrated by the dozens of beaten down people we meet every day. Yesterday when we were in the rural areas of Lowndes county, we talked about Freedom registration to one woman in a terrible house who said "I can't sign no paper." Lester then asked her "how will the pay for jobs and the homes ever get better unless we get together. Negroes have to do something to get something." She said, "I ain't no Negro, I'm a nigger. The Boss Man, he don't say nothing but nigger girl to me. I'm just a nigger, I can't sign no paper."

Meridian, Mid-summer

Last night, one of the boys said to his 6 year old brother, shortly after we had asked them why they didn't go home for supper: "Hey, Lance, tonite she'll be drunk & tomorrow he'll be drunk all day and we can get a lot of money out of them." (*He* & *she* being father & mother) . . . One day I watched a boy about 12 pick out very slowly and without a

62

single mistake, on the old typewriter at the community center:

The freedom we fight is for undrunks.

Indianola

. . . The interesting and horrible part of Negro life here is the absolute castration of the Negro male. He is trained to be nothing more than a child, with his . . . sheepish expression and "Yessir, yessir" to everything the white man says. Children must then emulate the mother who usually takes the aggressive, stronger role in the family. Few Negro boys can look to their fathers as a strong figure with which to identify . . .

Ruleville, July 2

The women make up the lion's share of the movement. This may be partially because they aren't as vulnerable economically but I don't think that factor is very important. Too many women work and oftentimes a man will get fired for the sins of his wife. Perhaps the major reason is that the women seem to have the calm courage necessary for a nonviolent campaign.

On July 2, the Civil Rights Act was signed by President Johnson. The volunteers regarded it with their new eyes and new knowledge. For this was the South, where 98.8 per cent of the Negroes were still in segregated schools ten years after a Supreme Court ruling; this was Mississippi, where 100 per cent of the Negroes still attended separate schools. This was also the state, one volunteer noted, where, when President Kennedy was shot, a police chief had declared a holiday and served fried chicken in the jail.

Dear Mom and Dad,   Clarksdale, July 3

Emotions in me are mixed now—watching that man who looks enough like Harry S. Truman to be his twin brother sign the civil rights bill—pride, joy, fear, disbelief, a wait-and-see streak. Thoughts of the thousands of Negroes, hundreds of thousands who will be helped by the bill, and the millions of poor to whom it will give dignity but no bread.

Watching the signing was a moment of happiness and a pain of hurt: people here in Clarksdale all know about that bill but tomorrow and Saturday, the 4th of July, they will still be in the cotton fields making three dollars a day. They'll still be in white homes working as maids, making three dollars a day. They'll still be starving and afraid.

I hurt more than I'm happy. . . . I know these people now and all I can say to them is vote, organize, starve.

Love,
Bob

Dear friends,   Greenwood, July

. . . It was rumored that some people would try to test the new bill. As most of you know, the Summer Project and SNCC decided not to test the bill. Mississippi is already a powder keg and it seemed foolish and dangerous to ignite it. We decided that the long range objectives of the project were more important than the short range objectives of eating a hamburger in a white grease-joint. . . .*

That next day we received a call from a local Negro, who said with such pride, even a little as if here had come her chance to be vindicated, "Ah'm going swimmin' in that pool; ah've waited a long time." We worked hard to convince her that a swim in the pool wasn't worth it, but it wasn't easy. How do you tell them to wait, if the law says they can? How do you convince them that the vote, education, and community awareness are more important than a lousy hamburger which to them symbolizes freedom? Yet somehow most of the local Negroes did become convinced and once again agreed to wait some more, a little longer. Where does their patience and faith come from? How much longer will it last? . . .

Best regards,
Phil

On the Fourth of July the volunteers had a holiday—but not to celebrate Independence Day nor the passing of the Civil Rights Bill. The project feared that antagonistic whites might take the occasion to demonstrate their "independence," so no work of any kind was attempted outside the offices that day. In several towns the local women cooked great quantities of food; there was picnicking and softball and the day became a feast for new friends.

*This decision was also based on the fact that testing would tie up too many summer workers and staff, both in general terms of time and personnel and because it might easily land people in jail. However, at least one project headquarters (in Clarksdale) did some unsuccessful testing with local people, mostly NAACP members.

We ate from two until five-thirty and every time we said we could eat no more we were served again with spicy chicken and this woman's or that woman's special ham and potato salad and sweetbread and corn bread and hot muffins and peas cooked in bacon and onion sauce and home-made applesauce and sodas and punches and grape juice and potato casseroles and more and more and more until the pies and the cakes and the ice cream came and we could not refuse. But the real part of this which makes it unforgettable for me were the many people who spoke of their gratitude for what we were doing. One woman said, "Most of all, these young white folks who are already free, they come here only to help us. They is proving to us that black and white can do it together, that it ain't true what we always thought, that all white folks is booger men, 'cause they sure is not." And people wonder why we came. . . .

They say in Mississippi
There are no neutrals found
You either Tom for Ross Barnett
Or else you are a man.
Oh, which side are you on, boy?
Which side are you on? . . .

Freedom Song

3 / That Long Walk to the Courthouse

Oxford, June 24

Howard Zinn says that Mississippi is not just a closed society, like the rest of the South. It is a locked society for which we must find the key. Many feel that the vote is the key and the number of votes the pressure on that key. All I can say is that I hope so. . . .

The Summer Project was a five-pronged assault on the status quo: 1) voter registration and organization of the new Mississippi Freedom Democratic Party; 2) the Freedom Schools; 3) community centers; 4) the white community project; 5) Federal programs research (to see how Negroes might obtain aid under existing or potential government arrangements). The volunteers worked on one or sometimes two of these programs; a small number were assigned to man the Project offices.

The first three programs formed the heart of the Project. They were interrelated, for the success of each depended on getting the Negro community organized and moving. The Project's basic idea was that in the absence of Federal action in Mississippi, the Negro had to lead his struggle for salvation himself; that to do so, he must find his own strength—and that the volunteers would aid him in this.

The largest number of volunteers were assigned to what they called VR—voter registration. They had two, simultaneous tasks: to help Negroes register in the conventional way, and to help build up the Freedom Democratic Party, a new

67

*political organization designed to give a voice to disenfran-
chised Negro voters. The Freedom party is described in Chapter
X. Regular VR meant, of course, registering in the way pre-
scribed by Mississippi law to vote for federal, state and local
officials. At the beginning of the summer, the volunteers con-
centrated on this aspect of political work.*

They had been briefed at Oxford.

Dear people,   June 25

Mississippi's eighty-two counties are divided in five congressional districts, and these districts serve as the frame for our
work. The first district is the northeastern part of the state;
Bob Moses describes this region geographically with the three
letters, TVA. The TVA has had some liberalizing influence
here. Also, the proportion of Negroes in the area rarely goes
over 30% in any county and is under 5% in one county. The
Negro farmers here are isolated from the mainstream of
thought and action and the problem of registration workers is
not so much the hostility of the local white citizens as it is
the difficulty of finding, educating, and bringing the unregis-
tered to the courthouse.

The Second Congressional district is the delta area, the land
of extensive plantations, and poor, dependent sharecroppers.
The Negro population here runs well over 60%. In the Second
district, the principal opposition to registration work comes
from the White Citizens Councils, and their main weapons
are economic here: one way or another, the majority of Negroes depends on the plantations for jobs and homes. Senator
Eastland's plantation in Sunflower County is in this region.

The Third Congressional district runs from the Second south
to Louisiana. This is mainly hill country, and our work here
is centered in five areas. Jackson, the capitol; Vicksburg,
which has had an indigenous voter registration drive since
the late forties and is generally considered "open"; Natchez
on the Mississippi, which has a large Armstrong tire and
rubber plant, and the whites there feel definitely threatened
by Negro labor (terrorism and brutality are believed to be
the work of white industrial workers in this area); McComb,
the capitol of Pike County, with a long record of brutality
and terrorism. Most Negroes in the Third district are small
farmers, and a high percentage own land. The danger in the
Third district, which is 40-50% Negro, comes from the re-
vived Ku Klux Klan.

The Fourth district, directly east of Jackson, is generally
considered the "easiest" in the state, but what happened in

HOLLY SPRINGS

BATESVILLE

TUPELO

CLARKSDALE

CHARLESTON
CLEVELAND

2

1

ABERDEEN

SHAW RULEVILLE
INDIANOLA
GREENVILLE

GREENWOOD
ITTA BENA

COLUMBUS
STARKVILLE

TCHULA
BELZONI

CARTHAGE
CANTON

PHILADELPHIA

FLORA

4

MERIDIAN

VICKSBURG
JACKSON

3

LAUREL

NATCHEZ

HATTIESBURG

McCOMB

5

GULFPORT BILOXI MOSS POINT
PASCAGOULA

• LOCATION OF MISSISSIPPI PROJECTS

CONGRESSIONAL DISTRICTS OF MISSISSIPPI

Philadelphia shows how relative that is. Negro population here runs under 50%.

The Fifth district runs south from Laurel to the coast. This area includes Hattiesburg and the Gulf Coast which has a large shipbuilding industry and tourism and is generally exposed to the outside world. The Negro population is under 33% and they don't have much trouble registering to vote on the coast. . . .

Jim

The voter registration workers learned that some of the places they would be going already had an active local movement while others would have to be "opened up." This meant first visiting the town from a nearby base; talking to the people to see who would go down to the courthouse to register; locating a place for meetings and if possible Negro homes in which to stay. The main goal was to find a few local Negroes willing to organize their neighbors and then carry on the struggle by themselves.

It was large order: according to the most reliable statistics, some 94 per cent of the eligible Negro voters in Mississippi weren't registered.

Valley View, August 25

The right to vote is completely controlled by the registrars —one to each of 82 counties. They alone decide whether an applicant has passed the test, they inform him only after a 30-day wait, and they don't have to tell him why he failed the test.

The registrar could always find a reason for flunking a Negro applicant: the undotted "i," a misspelling, or especially an error in question 19 which required the applicant to copy out and then interpret any one of the 286 sections of the Mississippi Constitution specified by the registrar. Some of the sections run as long as two pages, all in legalese. Negroes with Ph.D.'s were flunked, while white men with only a grammar school education were passed.

But more discouraging to the Negro than these technical traps was the fact that the names of all applicants were published in the newspaper for two weeks or more. It wasn't difficult to tell white and Negro names apart, as the white names were dignified by Mr., Miss, Mrs. And once identified . . .

. . . Fear of The Man, fear of Mr. Charlie . . . Occasionally it is the irrational fear of something new and untested. But usually it is a highly rational emotion, the economic fear of losing your job, the physical fear of being shot at. Domestic servants know that they will be fired if they register to vote; so will factory workers, so will Negroes who live on plantations. In Mississippi, registration is no private affair . . .

Dear Mom,   Holly Springs

When we walk up to a house there are always children out front. They look up and see white men in the car, and fear and caution cover their expressions. Those terrified eyes are never quite out of my mind; they drive me as little else could. The children run to their parents, hide behind them. We walk up, smile, say howdy, and hold out our hands. As we shake hands I tell them my name. They tell me their names and I say Mr.—, how do you do. It is likely the first time in the life of this farmer or housewife that a white man has shaken hands with them like that. This does not necessarily bode well to them. They think, if Mr. Charlie knew . . . Many are sharecroppers, who must turn over a third to a half of the year's harvest to a man who does no work at all, but who owns the land they till. They may be evicted, and have often been for far less serious offenses. Nearly everyone black in Mississippi is at least a year in debt. The threat of suspended credit and foreclosure is a tremendous burden. . . .

                                                      Love,
                                                      Bob

                                              Greenwood, July 15

We are trying to get people to go down to the courthouse to register. In Mississippi there are no deputy registrars, the only place that people can register is at the Courthouse at the County Seat. The county seat for Leflore County is Greenwood. This in itself restrains Negroes from voting because they don't like to go to the courthouse, which has bad connotations for them. Behind the courthouse is the Yazoo River. The river also has bad connotations; as Albert Darner said, it's "Dat river where dey floats them bodies in."

                                              Gulfport, July 8

Canvassing, the main technique in voter registration, is an

art, and like an art, it is not a scheduled thing. You don't work from 9 to 5. There is no such thing as a completed job until *everyone* is registered. When you cheat and take a lunch hour (and it feels like cheating) you suddenly find yourself reviewing a failure or a success to discover the whys: maybe I should have bullied him slightly, or maybe I should have talked less—and relied on silences. Did I rush him? Should I never have mentioned registering at all, and just tried to make friends and set him at ease? It goes on and on. . . .

Techniques and approaches vary. Mine is often like this:

Hi. My name is Steve M. (shake hands, having gotten name, address, from a mailbox). I'm with COFO. There are a lot of us working in this area, going from house to house trying to encourage people to go down and register to vote. (Pause). Are you a registered voter? (This is the direct technique. Often people, being afraid, will lie and say yes, but you can usually tell, because they will be very proud.) Are you planning on going down soon? (This makes them declare themselves. Usually they say "yes" or "I hadn't thought about it much." The other answer is "No, I ain't going down at all." "Well, I have a sample of the registration form." (Take it out and hand it to them.) "You know, some people are a little afraid to go down because they don't quite know what they're getting into. It's something new and different, and they're not sure about it."

Then I go on, "You know, it is so important that everyone get the vote. As it stands now, that man downtown in charge of roads doesn't have to listen to the Negroes. They can't put him out of office. He should be working *for* you." (Much gossip, chatter, mutual questions through all this).

Then pull out the Freedom Democratic Party application.

"This is a protest party. Anyone can join to protest the laws about voter registration and the way elections are carried out."

You get the picture. It goes on, 10 hours a day, 6 days a week. On Sundays we rest by working at other things. We go to church. Since all visitors are allotted time to speak, I relate voter registration to God. I have become a pretty good preacher. . . .

Few volunteers worked on canvassing the plantation workers; this perilous task was usually left to experienced staff members if attempted at all. But in Holmes County, a small group of volunteers developed a technique for doing it with the assistance of local Negro youths.

One can't move onto a plantation cold; or canvas a plantation in the same manner as the Negro ghetto in town. It's far too dangerous. Many plantations—homes included—are posted, meaning that no trespassing is permitted, and the owner feels that he has the prerogative to shoot us on sight when we are in the house of one of *his* Negroes.

Before we canvas a plantation, our preparation includes finding out whether the houses are posted, driving through or around the plantation without stopping, meanwhile making a detailed map of the plantation.

We're especially concerned with the number of roads in and out of the plantation. For instance, some houses could be too dangerous to canvas because of their location near the boss man's house and on a dead end road.

In addition to mapping, we attempt to talk to some of the tenants when they are off the plantation, and ask them about conditions. The kids often have contacts, and can get on the plantation unnoticed by the boss man, with the pretense of just visiting friends.

Our canvassing includes not only voter registration, but also extensive reports on conditions—wages, treatment by the boss man, condition of the houses, number of acres of cotton, etc. Much more such work needs to be done. The plantation system is crucial in Delta politics and economics, and the plantation system must be brought to an end if democracy is to be brought to the Delta. . . .

Love,
Joel

Sometimes people said "yes sir," they'd go down to the courthouse—and the volunteer felt they would have as easily said "no sir" if asked not to go down. It made no difference: they didn't go anyway. At the mass meetings, many would get all worked up with shouts of Freedom NOW, but do nothing when the time came. The fact that black Mississippi had become a land of children and old people—so many in between had gone north to escape—was a problem in many areas: "Senator Eastland needn't complain about all us idealists coming here, he's exiled all his in-state leaders." But there were Negroes of all ages who slammed the door in a volunteer's face when they heard the word "vote." And who could really blame them, when a police car was driving

*slowly by or the boss's brother was watching from the road—
or an Uncle Tom?*

Canton

The hardest of all to take are the "Uncle Toms," who sit in on our mass meetings, visit the homes we're staying in, gathering all the information they can to sell to the White Citizens Council. . . .

Clarksdale, July 9

One of the small Negro kids is a spy for Ben Collins, chief of police. He goes around listening to our talk all day, finds out where we live, and reports all we do every night. He calls himself Superman, and rumor has it that he is paid $3 a day for his services. He is only 12 years old.

Some of the "Toms" could be found among the Negro cops —a handful of men who were not permitted to arrest whites, weren't paid (except by the head, for each fellow Negro arrested) and had to buy their own uniforms.

Gulfport, June 24

While at the bar,* we started taking down names of local people who wanted to help us. One was a big lugubrious Negro man who said he was visiting from Chicago because he was bringing home the body of his dead wife. He was so dejected that I kept murmuring sympathetic phrases. Well—it turns out that he was a policeman who was following us. We're wondering whether to take him down to register . . .

And sometimes the volunteers ran into a very different sort of problem while trying to get the local people involved.

Ruleville, July 2

Mass meeting in the evening; Freedom songs, etc. Walking home in the dark, I was stopped by a young Negro man who began a conversation by asking me what went on in the mass meetings; he wanted precise details, where the money went,

---

* Mississippi is officially dry, with some dry-dry counties where beer is forbidden too, but semi-clandestine drinking goes on in many "cafe's." In places like Gulfport, on the coast, drinking is more open and volunteers canvassed the bars as well as stores and homes.

why do we sing so much? what do the people say? and so forth. He was persistent, forceful, and asking the most difficult questions. It came out that he wanted to join the Movement, but he couldn't understand non-violence. "I seen a picture in one of the books of this guy sitting on the ground, with his head down and his arms up, and this other fella was running and hit him on the ear like that. Just hit him. I don't get it. I couldn't do that." His voice was soft. I didn't see his face, it was dark, but we talked for almost two hours, walking . . .

Mass meetings were one of the main ways to get a community moving. People could then see that there were others who wanted their rights. But sometimes the fear in a community made it difficult just to get a church or hall for the gathering —and with some reason. Thirty-seven Negro churches were bombed or burned during the summer.

Como, August 18

"Good evening, Mr. Wallace."

"Good evenin'. Won't you come up and have a seat on the porch?"

"Don't mind if I do. That heat's something, isn't it?"

"Sure is. Water?"

"No, no thank you, sir. This shade is just fine. I didn't see you at the mass meeting last Thursday night."

"Well, I reckon you didn't. I *meant* to get out there, but Mrs. Wallace, you know, wasn't up to it. I hear it was a pretty good meetin', though."

"Well, you know, we had a lot of spirit there, but not too many people. Lots of young folks, but the adults just didn't turn out."

"That's the way it is—the young folks is always right out there runnin', and the older folks just sort of trot on behind."

"Well, we missed you, Mr. Wallace."

"I planned on bein' there. You countin' on having another meetin' soon?"

"That's one of the things I wanted to talk to you about, Mr. Wallace. I understand you're a deacon right here at the Baptist Church in town."

"That's right. Been a deacon there thirty-four years. My brother, George—you know—he's a deacon, too."

"Yes, sir. I've talked with him. How many deacons does your Church have?"

"There's seven now, I think. There's me, and there's George.

And then there's Henry Eastland, and Jimmy Stennis, and Mr. Howard out there east of town. Will Barnett lives down in Sardis, you know. Then H. K. Williams and Mr. Robertson right here in town."

"Yes. I've already spoken with Mr. Robertson. He said it would be all right with him if we organized a meeting up at your Church next week; but, of course, I'd have to speak to all the deacons first."

"Jack Robertson told you that?"

"Yes, sir, so I thought I'd come to see you, Mr. Wallace."

"Well, I'll give it to you just like it is. I'm with you one hundred per cent, and I'm plannin' on goin' down to the courthouse soon, you know. But speakin' for the Church, I'm not so sure about that."

"Why's that, sir?"

"Well, I guess just not yet. We're not ready for that yet, right here. But I'm with you one hundred per cent, and I think you're fine fellows doin' a fine job with our folks. The colored people around here have needed this for a long time."

"We're not really *doing* anything here, Mr. Wallace; it's you local people who have to do things, right here in Como, before the white man stomps you down. We're just here to let you know what we think can be done—by you."

"That's right!"

"And that's why we need to hold meetings, so we can talk to the people."

"That's right. What our people here need is education, and I think you're doing a fine job. That's what I tell all the folks around here when they talk against you. You're here to help us and we should do all we can."

"That's why we need your Church for a meeting, Mr. Wallace. We've held two meetings out of town now at Mountain Hill, and we'd like to talk to the people right here in town."

"I'm telling you now just the way it is; some of the white folks have been talkin' up against you all and your meetings now, and I don't want any trouble. I've been readin' about all them churches bein' burned and bombed . . ."

"But none of that has been here in Panola County, or anywhere around here. We've got the FBI watching here and Sheriff Hubbard has helped us out a couple of times."

"Well, I just don't want any trouble. You've been havin' your meetin's out at Mountain Hill—why can't you keep on havin' 'em there?"

"That's two miles out of town, Mr. Wallace, and we'd like to move into town, now, for our meetings. It's easier for the people who live here."

"Well, I just can't say yes."

"All right, Mr. Wallace. But Mr. Robertson said it was okay. So I think I'll talk to the other deacons. You haven't been down to the courthouse yet, sir?"

"No, but I'm plannin' on goin' down right soon now."

"Lots of people are going down this week. Maybe you could get a ride with Mr. Rice tomorrow."

"Well, not this week—but I'll be goin' down soon."

"All right, Mr. Wallace; I'll be back to talk to you again soon. I've got to be getting along now. I'll talk to the other deacons, and I hope to see you down at the courthouse soon, sir!"

"That's right! I'm with you one hundred per cent now. Good luck! And come on back."

Mr. Wallace represents a large number of people here in Como. Not everyone—far from it—but enough people think like him to make work occasionally exasperating, especially for the local people who are not "one hundred per cent *with us*" but who are working like hell to build a better Como for themselves . . . That "one hundred per cent with you" has become a joke with us. So much so that Mr. Howard, who went down with us to Batesville to register this morning, and who is going to be one of the stars of our mass meeting, said, as he left us this noon: "If I've passed that test, I'm with you two hundred per cent!"

In Indianola, the seat of Sunflower County (number of eligible Negroes registered: 2%, the ministers refused to lend their churches but a Negro Baptist Convention in the area voted unanimously to let the Project use a three-room brick schoolhouse. A mass meeting was called for July 23; no more than 100 local people were expected.

Dear Folks,   July 24

Last night was one of those times that are so encouraging and inspiring. We had a mass meeting in Indianola. Three weeks ago, there was no movement at all in that community. A few Project workers went in and began canvassing for registration. It was decided to set up a Freedom School. Another few workers went in as staff. In that short time they had generated enough interest and enthusiasm to bring out 350 people to the meeting!

I sat and watched faces that had been transformed with hope and courage. They were so beautiful, those faces. It is hard to put into words an experience like this. That sense of hope was so strong, so pervasive, each of us there felt with complete certainty that there can, there will, be a better world and a good life if we work for it. When James Forman speaks, he talks "soul-talk," reaching out to that part of us that is vital, that is creative, and the people respond with a radiance and a sureness that is so new to them. The word "new" is very significant—it not only means a change in the externals of their lives . . . the greatest import of "new" is the emerging "new value of themselves as human beings, with the right and will to act, to move, to shape their lives . . .

Love,

Ellen

There were other times, other places, when all the long hours of walking and talking seemed worthwhile.

McComb, August 20

The voter registration program, despite its shortcomings, is a beautiful thing to watch. Such a big step for these people! The voter registration classes are slightly tense, but what is more present is hope, positiveness. The people dress up carefully. They shake each other's hands, await eagerly the return of those who have gone down to the courthouse already. Two functional illiterates have come, and so many others have so much trouble filling out the form. But they're going down—a cemetery caretaker, a blind man, a cafe owner, a domestic . . .

Not only did people in a single town range from the fearful to the militant, but Negro communities as a whole varied from one part of the state to another. There was Greenville, for example, located on the Mississippi River; once a major port, it had been opened to the outside world . . .

Dad,   Greenville, August 9

Greenville is certainly a liberal city by Mississippi standards. It has three Negroes on its police force. The town appropriations to white and colored schools have each year come closer to being equal, and the police force watched the Klan as closely as COFO . . . The public library is integrated (after a small group of Negro high school students last year demonstrated and spent months in jail.) The Negro and white swimming pools are exactly alike. One of the town's leading

78

newspapers, Hodding Carter's *The Delta-Democratic Times,*
urges moderation and compliance with the law. In other
words, Greenville does not use terror tactics to maintain
segregation and it has come a bit closer than other cities in
Mississippi to making the separate but equal policy a reality.
In Illinois, a city like Greenville would be ultra-conservative
and would make even Winthrop Harbor seem a haven for
fanatic revolutionists. In Mississippi, it's liberal. . . .

Buzz

*Greenville, unlike the rest of the Delta, had a sizable Negro
middle class.*

Greenville, July 9

The whites here are darker than the colored sometimes,
making you wonder who should swim with whom. As for the
colored, I heard a little Negro girl saying scornfully to her
friend while touching her neck, "Oh Honey, you sure is
black."

July 14

The Negro leaders are of course the rich Negroes in town.
Many of them are afraid of their own position in the white
community and they don't want to move now that there are a
lot of people who want to move. . . . A lot of kids here take
a very cynical attitude toward the NAACP and even Martin
Luther King.

Hi,   Greenville, July 3

There is a group of approximately 150 high school boys
called the Mississippi Student Union. They've had a couple of
demonstrations and are eager to do something and pretty informed. This is where our big problem comes in. COFO told
us absolutely no demonstrating. Now we're faced with the
problem that if we don't support these kids in their demonstrations, we're not going to get the respect and cooperation
we need from them . . .

The old Negro leaders threatened to put an ad in the papers
branding us as Communists. It's a bad situation. A lot of the
poor Negroes who are just beginning to get active accuse the
old leaders of being directly under the thumb of the white
power structure (receiving bribes, etc.) . . . Your point in one
of your letters is certainly right, Mom. They are as much victims as others. But it seems they are in positions, and have

been, where they *could* work changes instead of blocking them. I hope we can reconcile . . .

Love,
Barb

Mileston, on the other hand, had a long tradition of violence; yet the situation in that little rural community was very different from most of Mississippi—for an unusual reason.

Dear Mom and Dad,   Mileston, July 6

Mileston, where I'm staying, is in the flat Delta section of Holmes County. The Negro farms here were once part of huge plantations. In 1939 the federal government confiscated the land when the plantation owners failed to pay back taxes, and the land was divided up among Negro families who had applied for it. Land reform (on a miniscule scale) has had an enormous effect on the people . . .

Last year Hollis Watkins, a SNCC staff member, began a voter registration drive here. He got about 14 Negroes to go to the court house with the intention of registering to vote. Sheriff Smith greeted the party with a six shooter drawn from his pocket, and said "Okay, who's first?" Most of the Negroes remained cautiously quiet. After several seconds a man who had never before been a leader stepped up to the Sheriff, smiled and said, "I'm first, Hartman Turnbow." All registration applications were permitted to be filled out and all were judged illiterate. The next week, Turnbow's house was bombed with Molotov cocktails. When the Turnbows left the burning house, they were shot at, and they shot back until the attackers fled. A couple of days later, Mr. Turnbow, Hollis Watkins, Robert Moses and a couple of other people were arrested for arson; Turnbow was accused of having bombed his own house which wasn't insured. Sheriff Smith was the one witness against them. Mr. Turnbow was convicted in a Justice of Peace Court, but the conviction was overruled in a federal district court . . .

The Negro people we are living with have enormous hope and are extremely practical about achieving their goals. This community is an oasis of hope in a desert of broken minds: the plantation sharecroppers who have little reason for hope . . .

Love,
Joel

Both Greenville and Mileston had some history of civil rights action. The town of Drew, also in the Delta, was a new experience: volunteers had to "open it up," commuting there from nearby Ruleville where Mrs. Fannie Lou Hamer lived.

A 24-year-old white volunteer from Philadelphia who had been a youth worker with the Quakers tells part of the story of Drew in a series of letters.

Dear friends,   Ruleville, June 24

Last evening we went up to Drew, the tough little town north of here to do some canvassing. Whites streamed through the area . . . sometimes they would call a Negro over to their car and send him scampering back in his house. The police kept talking into their mikes as they cruised by. Most of the [Negro] people were not at all receptive. I talked for a while to some kids who may be willing to start a group. We talked about the whole movement and about how you were safer if the community was united. This evening we will go back again and talk to the people a bit, just to show them we are still around. . . .

July 2

There were still a lot of folks who didn't want to have anything to do with it all because it meant trouble. I met a very tall freshman at the local high school who said he wasn't afraid of the "man." As I walked down the road with him, his mother came to warn him not to get mixed up with us. She said they probably wouldn't hurt *us* but would beat *him* as soon as we had left. She told me she was afraid for her boys. She wants to raise them safely and get them out of here . . . There was an old couple, married 62 years, who said they couldn't pull much any more but still could push. This seems to be the sentiment of many of the people in this town. They would be willing to take a step but they don't want to be first. We are gradually getting a list of about half a dozen people who say they are now willing to go down to the courthouse. . . .

July 11

I drove up to Drew to see if the one-legged WWI veteran was ready to go to the courthouse to register. He said he was ready at any time, though he had lost his glasses and so couldn't read very well. I assured him that the important thing was to take the stand of going down . . . It will help

81

the Justice Dept. case against this registrar to have as many people attempt to register as possible. I accompanied Mr. K., a proud 70-year-old, into the courthouse. We were informed that the registrar was out for a while and that I would have to leave as soon as he came back. I suggested that Mr. K. take the empty seat but he was reluctant to risk a rebuke by sitting "out of bounds." We stood there for ten minutes. Finally the registrar came in and asked me if I intended to help Mr. K. register. I said, "no," and asked him if Mr. K. could have a seat. He said "of course." Our hesitancy in this instance had not been warranted, but what about next time?

I sat out on the porch of the columned courthouse and waited. It didn't take long. The print was so fine that Mr. K. couldn't make much out of it. We went over to a Negro cafe for a pop and then I left to do some canvassing. Mr. K. assured me that the 2 hour wait [to ride back with me] wouldn't bother him. The fight for freedom needs a lot of patience, he thought, and that was one thing he was strong on.

I also met a guy who said that the preacher told the people not to mess with us. We got into a long biblical argument about whether people should sit around and get along as best they could while waiting on the Lord or try to change things to more nearly meet his design. I think I got the best of the argument, but then he talked about how well he got on with the white folks. He said, "Why it was just the other day that Mayor Williford congratulated me for being a good Negro." I could see that he had so deeply identified with the present system and the ways it left open for Negroes to get ahead that he wasn't open to ideas of change. The Negro kids I was canvassing with were disgusted. The man's wife gave me a sort of whimsical smile from the door. I read it (maybe wishfully) to mean "You can't talk any sense into that old man."

A number of people in Drew seem to resent our forays. It is crucial that we get a place for meetings there and have some people stay there for a week or two. Now we are planning an open-air meeting for next week. I hope it will get things off the ground.

The day of the first mass meeting in Drew arrived: Tuesday, July 14.

July 18

. . . Four of us went to distribute flyers announcing the meeting. I talked to a woman who had been down to register a

82

week before. She was afraid. Her husband had lost his job. Even before we got there a couple of her sons had been man-handled by the police. She was now full of wild rumors about shootings and beatings, etc. I checked out two of them later. They were groundless. This sort of rumor-spreading is quite prevalent when people get really scared. . . .

At 6 P.M. we returned to Drew for the meeting, to be held in front of a church (they wouldn't let us meet inside, but hadn't told us not to meet outside). A number of kids collected and stood around in a circle with about 15 of us to sing freedom songs. Across the street perhaps 100 adults stood watching. Since this was the first meeting in town, we passed out mimeoed song sheets. Fred Miller, Negro from Mobile, stepped out to the edge of the street to give somebody a sheet. The cops nabbed him. I was about to follow suit so he wouldn't be alone, but Mac's policy [Charles McLaurin, SNCC project director] was to ignore the arrest. We sang on mightily "Ain't going to let no jailing turn me around." A group of girls was sort of leaning against the cars on the periphery of the meeting. Mac went over to encourage them to join us. I gave a couple of song sheets to the girls. A cop rushed across the street and told me to come along. I guess I was sort of aware that my actions would get me arrested, but felt that we had to show these girls that we were not afraid. I was also concerned with what might happen to Fred if he was the only one.

. . . The cop at the station was quite scrupulous about letting me make a phone call. I was then driven to a little concrete structure which looked like a power house. I could hear Fred's courageous, off-key rendition of a freedom song from inside and joined him as we approached. He was very happy to see me. Not long thereafter, four more of our group were driven up to make their calls . . .

The Drew jail consists of three small cells off a wide hall. It was filthy, hot and stuffy. A cop came back to give us some toilet paper. We sang songs for a while, and yelled greetings to Negroes who drove by curiously. One of the staff workers had been in jail 106 times. I asked the cop if he could open another cell as there were not enough beds accessible to us. He mumbled something about how that would be impossible and left. They hadn't confiscated anything and one of the guys had a battered copy of *The Other America*, so we divided up the chapters. I got the dismal one on the problems of the aged . . . To be old and forgotten is certainly a worse sentence than mine (I wouldn't recommend that book for those planning to do time) . . .

Well, the night was spent swatting mosquitoes. An old Negro couple walked by in front of the jail and asked how we were doing. They said they supported us and the old lady said, "God bless you all." This, in the context of a tense town with a pretty constant stream of whites in cars driving by. . . .

The group was released the next day after paying $100 bail apiece on a charge of unlawful distribution of literature. In order that the black people of Drew would not think the arrest of seven workers could stop the Movement in their town, a second mass meeting had been called for that same night. At 4:30 A.M., while the seven were still in jail, volunteers distributed announcements to the Drew plantation workers before they went to the fields for the day.

The meeting began to roll about 6 P.M. on July 15.

July 27

. . . When we got there we found the group, a much larger group than the night before, with a considerable number of adults, singing on the lot next to the church grounds. (The police had put pressure on the deacons to deny us the use of the church grounds.) There were deputies in great profusion this time, in their white helmets. The street had been barricaded off, but there was still a large crowd watching from the other side of the street. Mac was making a forceful speech . . . Just then the cop came up with an old lady who said she owned the lot we were meeting on. The chief called Mac over to the car and the lady told him the niggers didn't want us around. Mac said that all who wanted to stand for freedom should meet in the street. I held back, but when I saw so many local people taking that courageous step, I was drawn to support them. The deputies marched us off to the little jail we had left just that morning.

This time the place was pretty crowded. There were about ten of us plus 5 kids from the Ruleville Student Movement and ten local people. There was one high school boy from Drew who had been on his way to football practice, about 6 ladies in their thirties who were worried a bit about their families but were generally quite solid. . . .

Well, it took them over an hour to decide where to send us all and how to get us there but finally we set out in a long convoy, first to the county farm to let off the Negro men and women, and then on to the county jail to let off the whites. We were a bit scared about the prospects of landing in a cell with a bunch of whites, so we ditched our SNCC pins.

We were marched up to the second floor by a Negro jailer and put in a cell with one white prisoner. The cell was very small with three double bunks, one of the beds had no mattress and was strewn with the refuse of past boarders. We told the guy that we had been picked up for standing in the street and bitched profusely about the injustice. He had been there a week. Was picked up, he said, for drinking two beers, charged with disturbing the peace and sentenced to a month at the county farm. He was endowed with this typical attitude toward Negroes but had some very healthy grievances against the system down here and I think we might have made some progress with him if we hadn't been so cautious about revealing our identity. . . .

Best,
Mike

Again they were released the next day. By now, bail for those arrested had mounted to almost $4000. More dollars were being put in the town coffers than new voters on the rolls. And so it went in most parts of the state.

In some counties, suits had been brought against the registrar to stop discriminating against Negro applicants. The federal injunctions or court orders which followed promised to give the potential Negro voter a real chance. One of these had been issued in Panola County, in northern Mississippi, which has a 56 per cent Negro population. There were two county seats there instead of the usual one—Sardis and Batesville—and after the court order, the registrar's office in Sardis closed. So Batesville became a center of activity. It had a twenty-year-old tradition of local people taking the initiative; their Voters' League had filed the suit which led to the court order of 1964. Two of Batesville's leaders were Robert J. Miles and his wife.

June 30

. . . He is a Negro farmer who owns his own land (about 600 acres as I understand). He has a college education as do all his children. A quiet, humble fellow with a great sense of humor. He thinks out his moves carefully and doesn't take any crap from the white man . . .

. . . Mrs. Miles had a great comment on the town swimming pool which is, of course, not integrated. She said, "I don't see why they won't let us swim in the pool. It's been proven we don't fade."

The volunteers started working the town. One of the first targets was the teachers, always the hardest group to get moving. As county employees, they had to take an oath swearing that they did not belong to the NAACP—among other "subversive" organizations.

Dear people, Batesville, July 9

The good colored people of Panola County support five high schools, with a total faculty of a few over one hundred. Of all the people who have already registered to vote in the county, there have been no teachers. We are trying to get the teachers to register in a special campaign. Everyone is willing to go to the courthouse—after someone else . . .

Just before COFO moved into Batesville the county colored teachers were given a slight raise in salary. The contracts are to be signed this week—maybe. We have finally assembled a group of twelve to fifteen teachers who promised to go to the courthouse next Saturday, contract or no contract . . .

Jim

The principal of the Negro school (1 through 12 in the same building) here in Batesville is no help. We are going to get a group of teachers together without him, and have them go down in a group. If any one is fired, all will be, and we are told by the local Justice Dept. man that we could have a quick suit. I interviewed the principal myself. He sat in his air-conditioned house and talked about how he didn't want any "fanfare." Next door a family of 8 or 10 sat in front of one of the worst looking shacks I've seen down here . . .

July 23

. . . Finally last Saturday, having studied their strategy carefully, five teachers went to register together. Four of them are young and energetic and certain that they could find a job elsewhere. One of them is a dynamic widow with ten children and a patch of land. She could not possibly afford to lose her job. Their courage has paid off. In the five days since the group went, teachers have been going to the courthouse at the rate of three a day. Yesterday, to the surprise and delight of the entire community, the Principal registered.

The teachers did not lose their contracts. And the Negroes of Panola ceased to dread the publication of their names in the newspaper.

. . . In Panola County now the Negro citizens look with pride at their names in the Panolian; they point out the names of friends and neighbors and hurry to the courthouse to be enlisted on the honor roll.

Meanwhile, voter registration workers had spread out into other towns of Panola County like Como and Cranshaw. Registration was going well. Too well, for the white folk of Batesville.

Batesville, August 1

We're all a little nervous. Four COFO workers—including me—are staying with the Robert Miles' on their farm just outside of Batesville. Mrs Miles' 25 yr. old son Robert Jr. is stationed out in the yard with a gun. (Yes, the Movement is still non-violent; but every farmer—white and black—in the Delta has a gun. Mr. Miles has seven, all loaded.)

Things are getting very tense around here. Last night, while I was eating a peanut butter sandwich in the kitchen and talking to the other white girl staying here, two shots whizzed right by the kitchen window—I could even see a flash of light from the gun.

Since last Saturday night when the Miles' house was bombed with a tear gas grenade, several other Negroes in town have received bomb threats. . . .

We think that the heightened tension is pretty much a testimonial to the success of our voter registration drive. About 500 Negroes have registered since the summer volunteers arrived in Batesville—this in a county where until recently only two Negroes had been able to register in seventy years . . .

But the Panola story was unique. Tallahatchie County also had an injunction; two Negroes attempted to register that summer for the first time since Reconstruction—with five carloads of F.B.I. men standing by for the occasion. In Madison County volunteers found that economic intimidation made the injunction virtually worthless.

There are 82 counties in the state of Mississippi; rulings against the registrar would have to be obtained in 82 separate suits—and that was only a first step. An omnibus ruling *against all registrars had been rejected by a federal court in Mississippi.* As Martin Luther King pointed out in a speech, even at slightly better than the present rate, it would take a hundred and thirty-five years to register half of the eligible Negroes.*

Jackson, August 14

Until I got here, I didn't fully realize how much is needed and how long and slow everything goes. The one complaint that is most often heard is, "Where is the Justice Department?"

---

* In March, 1965, the Supreme Court overruled this decision and upheld the power of the Justice Department to sue a state in order to enforce voting rights.

4 / School for Freedom

Greenwood, July

All day long the older people sit stilly on their porches.
The hand that occasionally moves to fan is almost accidental,
even miraculous. When we walk down the street we walk a
kind of gauntlet between these porch-sitters. Out of the dull
resentment and the weary suspicion that is directed not so
much at us (for they all seem to know our mission) as at
the railroad tracks, at the street itself, come the words and
the tone that are always shocking: "How you all? . . . Jes'
fine, thanky', jes' fine!" Always an artificial, pious enthusiasm,
until it seems a ventriloquist's trick. And I always find it a
parody of the behavior that white supremacy has enforced
on the Negro.

But lo, brown and black and cream-colored children fill
the street with a marvelous vitality. The smallest of them has
an air of authority and self-reliance about him, has a sure
knowledge of the game at hand; and he always, always stands
up for his rights. If you view the scene of porch and street
as a timeless version of the range of a single generation,
then that boy, free, running, yelling, is simultaneously that
old man fading into death, submitting to it, on the shaded
porch. Because between the street and the house something
important has died, something has been killed.

I think this kind of image, and the possibility of a variation
on it, is at the heart of the momentousness that all of us
teaching in the Freedom School are beginning to feel. . . .
Our purpose is to expand awareness, to fortify what the student already knows—although inarticulately—that he is a
human being and deserving of respect . . .

Dear people,   Ruleville, July

Mississippians often boast that more money has been spent

on Negro schools in the last ten years than on white schools. This is true, at least with one qualification: *capital expenditures* on Negro schools have exceeded those on white schools. On annual per pupil operating expenditures, the white schools are still way ahead. The reason for this tremendous increase in capital expenditure is simple: they are starting from scratch because there were hardly any Negro schools before. Every Negro school you see is new, but that is not because of the white Mississippian's generosity towards "his Nigras." It is because of the Supreme Court decisions of 1954 and 1955. The South is finally trying to carry out the letter of the Plessy vs. Ferguson, "separate but equal" decision of 1896.

However, with this "step forward" came what is perhaps an even more vast step backward: the abolition of compulsory education in 1956, still in effect. That was done to prepare for the setting up of private schools, as in Prince Edward County, Virginia. It has already hurt one generation of Negroes, who, just as schools were finally being set up, have in many cases been enticed away from the schools to work in the fields.

But let's see what kind of schools they have been enticed away from. After lengthy talks with several teachers and many students, I feel able to reach some conclusions. First of all, those brand new buildings are shells. In Shaw, for instance the following things found in the white school are missing from the Negro school: lockers of any kind (even for the football team), ventilators, central heating (they have those electric fan units in the ceiling such as you see in garages), water coolers (there is one cooler for 1800 students), bleachers for the football games, a school car of any kind, landscaping or anything else to make the school pleasant. Children get textbooks discarded by the white schools. Shop equipment and typewriters for business courses come the same way. Perhaps it is what Aaron Henry called "Mississippi's affinity for the bottom" that we are fighting . . .

Charles

Greenville

The training of teachers in Mississippi is, to make a crude understatement, inadequate. To begin with, these teachers are themselves products of Mississippi grade schools and high schools. The qualifications for teachers are low at all levels, including college. The Negro colleges are understaffed, under-equipped, underpaid, under everything. Many of the Negro teachers in Greenville went to college at MVC (Mississippi Vocational College), which isn't even accredited outside of Mississippi . . . The schools of Greenville are all segregated, and Greenville just can't afford to operate two school systems on an equal basis . . .

Carthage, August 9

. . . I couldn't begin to describe the condition of their 25¢ school bus. Last year the bus had no heat and no windows. If children are picked up at 7:30 A.M. they often didn't make it to school until after 12:30 P.M. Several times when the bus broke down the children would have to walk to a farmhouse to warm up. Then when they get to school they are supposed to get an equal education.

Some of the Negro high schools weren't even dignified with the name, but called Attendance Centers. "And I gather that attendance is indeed the major content of the school day," wrote one volunteer . . .

Canton

Yesterday I decided to find out just how much they (mostly 6th & 7th graders), knew about our federal government. When I got discouraged by the blank looks on their faces, I asked, "What is the capital of the United States?" "Jackson?" . . . "How many states are there in the U.S.?" "? ? . . 82?" (82 counties in Miss.) Is this symbolic?

Hattiesburg

. . . The students are taught nothing of their heritage. The only outstanding Negroes they are told about are Booker T. Washington and George Washington Carver. They learn nothing of the contributions Negroes have made to our culture or anything else which could give them any reason to disbelieve the lies they are told about Negroes being unable to do anything worthwhile . . .

Mound Bayou

The county superintendent of schools ordered that neither foreign languages nor civics shall be taught in any Negro schools, nor shall American history from 1860 to 1875 be taught . . .

91

My students are from 13 to 17 years old, and not one of them had heard about the Supreme Court decision of 1954. I don't need to tell them that segregation is wrong, and that separate-but-equal is a myth; but they are surprised to hear that the law is on their side, because they hear only about the laws of Mississippi in their schools. . . .

The Negro response to the opening of the Freedom Schools was dramatic: by midsummer, 41 schools with 2165 pupils had been established. In Hattiesburg, it wasn't a response but an onslaught.

Saturday, July 4

. . . All this week we have been working on curriculum, schedules, registration of students and assembling materials for the Freedom Schools at Hattiesburg. It became evident quite early that we were going to have many more than the expected 75 students. We called Jackson and got a promise of more teachers—at full strength we will have 23. This was when we expected 150 students. On registration day, however, we had a totally unexpected deluge: 600 students! They were expecting only 700 for the whole state. After a while, as they were coming in, it changed from a celebration to a crisis. This is 26 students per teacher—much better than the local or usual ratios, but still not enough (like 5 to 1) to do all we want to in six weeks. Somehow we must set up a complete school system: 6 churches as schools spread around the city (which makes a huge transportation problem for teachers); next to nothing in materials; an age range from 8 to 82. . . .

We have been here only a week and we must set up this system before Monday when school starts, but we will do it; in fact the thought that we might not make it hasn't even occurred to us. The point here, as I told a curious white Baptist minister on registration day, is that the Negroes of Hattiesburg *do* want to study and learn. . . .

The Freedom Schools stood for everything which the regular schools had discouraged. They were a sort of mental revolution, requiring special tactics: a "citizenship curriculum" in which reading, writing and speaking skills would be developed through discussion of Negro history, literature, the Movement, and the Mississippi power structure. All the pupils had a session of this course, which went by different names at different projects, and then they chose from more academic subjects for the rest of their time in school— algebra, chemistry, biology, whatever they asked to have taught. The evening classes for adults offered health, literacy, and typing classes, again with an emphasis on life as the Negroes knew it.

Dear Mom and Dad: Holly Spring

The atmosphere in class is unbelievable. It is what every teacher dreams about—real, honest enthusiasm and desire to learn anything and everything. The girls come to class of their own free will. They respond to everything that is said. They are excited about learning. They drain me of everything that I have to offer so that I go home at night completely exhausted but very happy. . . .

I start out at 10:30 teaching what we call the Core Curriculum, which is Negro History and the History and Philosophy of the Movement, to about fifteen girls ranging from 15 to 25 years of age. I have one girl who is married with four children, another who is 23 and a graduate from a white college in Tennessee, also very poorly educated. The majority go to a Roman Catholic High School in Holly Springs and have therefore received a fairly decent education by Mississippi standards. They can, for the most part, express themselves on paper but their skills in no way compare to juniors and seniors in northern suburban schools.

In one of my first classes, I gave a talk on Haiti and the slave revolt which took place there at the end of the eighteenth century. I told them how the French government (during the French Revolution) abolished slavery all over the French Empire. And then I told them that the English decided to invade the island and take it over for a colony of their own. I watched faces fall all around me. They knew that a small island, run by former slaves, could not defeat England. And then I told that the people of Haiti succeeded in keeping the English out. I watched a smile spread slowly over a girl's face. And I felt girls sit up and look at me intently. Then I told them that Napoleon came to power, reinstated slavery, and sent an expedition to reconquer Haiti. Their faces began to fall again. They waited for me to tell them that France defeated the former slaves, hoping against hope that I would say that they didn't. But when I told them that the French generals tricked the Haitian leader Toussaint to come aboard their ship, captured him and sent him back to France to die, they knew that there was no hope. They waited for me to spell out the defeat. And when I told them that Haiti did succeed in

93

keeping out the European powers and was recognized finally as an independent republic, they just looked at me and smiled. The room stirred with a gladness and a pride that this could have happened. And I felt so happy and so humble that I could have told them this little story and it could have meant so much.

We have also talked about what it means to be a Southern white who wants to stand up but who is alone, rejected by other whites and not fully accepted by the Negroes. We have talked about their feelings about Southern whites. One day three little white girls came to our school and I asked them to understand how the three girls felt by remembering how it feels when they are around a lot of whites. We agreed that we would not stare at the girls but try to make them feel as normal as possible.

Along with my Core class I teach a religion class at one every afternoon and a class on non-violence at four-fifteen. All my classes are approximately an hour. Both these classes are made up of four to six girls from my morning class and about four boys of the same age group. In religion they are being confronted for the first time with people whom they respect who do not believe in God and with people who believe in God but do not take the Bible literally. It's a challenging class because I have no desire to destroy their belief, whether Roman Catholic or Baptist, but I want them to learn to look at all things critically and to learn to separate fact from interpretation and myth in all areas, not just religion.

Every class is beautiful. The girls respond, respond, respond. And they disagree among themselves. I have no doubt that soon they will be disagreeing with me. At least this is one thing that I am working towards. They are a sharp group. But they are under-educated and starved for knowledge. They know that they have been cheated and they want anything and everything that we can give them.

I have a great deal of faith in these students. They are very mature and very concerned about other people. I really think that they will be able to carry on without us. At least this is my dream . . .

Love,
Pam

Indianola, August 17

I can see the change. The 16-year old's discovery of poetry, of Whitman and Cummings and above all, the struggle to express thoughts in words, to translate ideas into concrete written words. After two weeks a child finally looks me in the eye, unafraid, acknowledging a bond of trust which 300 years of Mississippians said should never, could never exist. I can feel the growth of self-confidence . . .

Biloxi, Aug. 16

In the Freedom School one day during poetry writing, a 12-year old girl handed in this poem to her teacher:

What Is Wrong?

What is wrong with me everywhere I go
No one seems to look at me.
Sometimes I cry.

I walk through woods and sit on a stone.
I look at the stars and I sometimes wish.

Probably if my wish ever comes true,
Everyone will look at me.

Then she broke down crying in her sister's arms. The Freedom School here had given this girl the opportunity of meeting someone she felt she could express her problems to . . .

Dear Mom and Dad, Meridian, Midsummer

The Freedom School is an old Baptist Seminary, which was supposed to be condemned last year. We are thankful for it. We are one of the few Freedom Schools with a building of our own and classrooms and desks and blackboards. I teach two sections of a course called Freedom and the Negro in America—we talk about things like "What do we mean when we say, 'Things are bad in Mississippi?' " "What do white people have that we want?" "What do they have that we don't want?" And I am teaching French to the younger kids— mostly 11 to 14. I never expected to come to Mississippi to teach French, but they love it. As it is not taught at all in the Negroes' school, and is taught in white schools, it is a symbol of what they do not receive in school. And it turns out to be a good way to develop grammar and phonetic skills that would bore them in English, and to do some desperately needed broadening of cultural horizons . . .

Love,
Gail

. . . One thing that I've found here is that the students are on a much higher level than I had been led to expect. A lot of books which I wouldn't think of bringing because they would be "on too high a level" or "too intellectual" are being used very successfully. If reading levels are not always the highest, the "philosophical" understanding is almost alarming: some of the things that our 11 and 12 year olds will come out with would never be expected from someone of that age in the North. . . .

Harmony, July 20

. . . My History of Religion course is going fine—they are extremely interested in Judaism, in the fact that I am a Jew, in the rituals and beliefs of Judaism, etc. By this week, I hope to get into the origins of christianity in Judaism so that they can all (about 12) get a deeper feeling for the roots of Catholicism, and in turn the roots of their *own* faith, Southern Baptist. . . .

August 19

Wednesday I went with a bunch of Freedom School kids to Biloxi where we saw *In White America*. A touring company has been formed this summer to play all over the state.* I guess you know what the play is about—a symposium on the Negro in America. It is pretty strong stuff—what the slave ships were like, what being a slave was like, the lynchings, Father Divine in the 30's, Little Rock, and an added scene: a speech by Rita Schwerner.

This was the first theater most of these people had ever seen. They didn't have theater manners yet and it was great. They shouted, "Sho nuff" and "You said it" when they agreed with something and joined in singing the songs. One of the actresses said, "You can't imagine what it was like under slavery" and a 15-year old girl next to me said, "Oh, yes I can."

* The Free Southern Theatre, conceived in the spring of 1964 by several SNCC workers. With an integrated company of eight, it gave Martin Duberman's play in thirteen communities.

Most of last week was spent working on the "Clarksdale Freedom Press." Getting all the interested kids in the basement of Haven Methodist Church, examining possible articles, editing them, typing them, etc., was great! The place looked just like a newspaper office with people running in and out, with typewriters going, and newsprint everywhere. It was excellent experience for the kids too . . . They did most of the work and made most of the decisions. . . .

Many of the schools mimeographed such newspapers, using material written by the students: reportage, political essays, poetry—always about themselves and their feelings as Negroes and how to change things for the better. But along with this kind of success, each Freedom School had its own problems and each teacher his discouraging experiences.

Dear John and Cleo,   Canton, July 10-16

I'm sitting in what we've turned into a Freedom School—a one room wooden church . . . Most of the windows are half paneless. The only seats resemble picnic benches. One lamp, hung from the ceiling . . . A colored U.S. map, a few Freedom posters, some prints torn from an old calendar have brightened the room a little since we came. A broom and a scrub brush helped, too, to dispel the terrible depression that fell over my two fellow teachers and me when we first saw the place. That depression got heavier before it became lighter, though. On registration day nobody came and we had our scrubbed benches, clean floors and brightened walls all to ourselves. For several days after, we combed the area for students. Some were holding back out of fear—their own and/or their parents' (this building was bombed a month ago; the police have been circling it almost hourly since we moved into it); many distrusted us; some simply didn't care. But by some mysterious force which I really don't understand, a few people began appearing for classes, averaging about 20 a day now—never the same 20. I don't know how meaningful or lasting a response we're getting overall. Somedays I'm kind of thrilled; other days bring bitter discouragement. . . .

Love,

Jo

Indianola

Naturally they hardly trust whites and there is a lot of 'Yes Ma'am' and constant agreement with what you say. Until a

97

week and a half ago, these children had never seen a white woman get down on her hands and knees and scrub a floor. . . .

The Summer Project has two Freedom Schools in Palmer's Crossing, a rural community about two miles outside of Hattiesburg. The two schools have nine teachers, five of them (including myself) professionals. It has been rough. Much of what we know about teaching must be unlearned or relearned here. The standard academic approach has not worked at all well, even when material has been simplified . . . The kids we are dealing with are not trained to listen to and absorb information presented in an organized, "logical," manner . . . The students do not seem to be able to follow a point-by-point presentation at all, whether simple or complex. They learn by talking, by conversation, by rambling around and beating the nearby bushes. And they learn by acting things out.

We have rather small children (aged 8 and up), and these are our worst problems. Once when it was my turn to babysit I tried to hold a lesson on politics. None of the little kids knew what politics or government were, so I asked them if they knew what the mayor is. Someone volunteered that the mayor is sort of like a horse. (This led to a spelling lesson on "mayor" and "mare"). In order to get down to real basics, I asked if anyone had ever seen a street or road. Yes, they had. How, I asked, did they think streets and roads got there? Who made them? Here the civics lesson came to an end. "God," a little girl replied. A lengthy theological discussion followed. "Does God make trees?" "Yes." "Do people make trees?" "No." "Does God make houses?" "Yes." "Do people make houses"? "No. God makes everything." This position seemed unassailable by logic alone, so, thinking that something massive must be done at once, I asked a few of the more sober-minded boys if they had ever seen someone build a house. Indeed they had, and I launched them on a long description of how this is done, making sure that real people figured prominently in the description. It was not without interest, but it wasn't a civics lesson.

One day we listened to the recording of "In White America" . . . The kids were struck by the incident in the Little Rock integration riots, in which a small Negro girl describes movingly how she was spit on and cursed as she tried to go to the previously all white school. Our discussion soon came to examine the purposes of school integration. All the kids were totally convinced that integration will mean that they would get schooling as good as the whites. It was, for them, a very simple point: Negro schools, in hundreds of little ways, are not as good as white schools.

I tried to make the question more theoretical. Suppose Mississippi should decide to spend as much money on Negro education as it does on white, so that the two schools would really be equal. Would they still favor integrated schools? For some of the kids this possibility was too incredible to accept seriously. They could not imagine Mississippi making Negro schools equal. But others saw that the point of the question was whether integration has a value in itself, apart from the equality it would bring. Few kids seemed ever to have thought of it just that way, but a little prompting gave them an idea. Did they think that Negroes and whites in Mississippi really understood each other? There was a chorus of deeply felt Noes. They quite frankly admitted not understanding white people any better than white people understood them. Did they think this would be true if whites and Negroes had been going to school together all their lives? Probably not. I was then able to get in a philosophic point about education. Education, I said, is supposed to give people an understanding of what the world is really like. A school system that closes students off to half the people in their world cannot do this. And so segregation deprives whites equally with Negroes. . . .

Dear Friends: Meridian, July 7 & 15

Today was the second day of full operation at the Meridian Freedom School. In one way, it has been a tremendous success; so far, we have probably had about a hundred and twenty students register (we were only expecting about 50 or so), and that only includes students over 12 years of age. Partially because the school is entirely voluntary, and partially because there is no punishment or even threat arising from lateness or absence or noise, there is virtually no discipline problem. Everyone seems to be having a good time (except, of course, the teachers).

The unfortunate results are that we have tended to set up a somewhat formal structure (with, malheureusement, even bells between classes). The classes tend to be larger than the five or six students that were originally planned: yesterday there were 38 students in my math class and 41 in my French class. The result is a slowly emerging super-bureaucracy, and a tendency toward more "conventional" methods of teaching (this latter being helped along somewhat by some of our "professional" teachers, who have a condescending attitude toward the rest of us; the remark, "Well, you don't know because you're not a *professional*" has more than once wafted from their lips.) ...

Best,
Pete

Teachers in the Delta and other cotton growing areas faced a special problem: the split shift.

Indianola, August 9

The Negro schools in the Delta are open from early Nov. until late May. Then the schools close so the kids can chop cotton for Mr. Charley. In the middle of June, they open again and the kids go to school from 8 until 2:30. Then in Sept., when all the whites go back to school, the Negro schools close so that the children can pick cotton until November. Talk about King Cotton!

Since it wasn't chopping or picking time, the regular schools were open and Freedom School classes could start only after three o'clock. For this and other reasons, a crisis evolved in Shaw [Bolivar County] shortly after volunteers went there from nearby Ruleville to set up a school. "Shaw," a SNCC report had told the volunteers, "is a depressing little town uselessly and stupidly stuck in the middle of the cotton fields . . ."

July

. . . We aren't reaching the kids. They go to school now from seven until one o'clock and they want to sleep, not to have more study in the blazing heat of the Mississippi sun and dust. So would I in their place. Furthermore, they don't see how we can help them to be free. At this point, neither do we. Slow change is unthinkable when so much change is needed, when there is so much hurt . . .

We have cast about for a way to allow the Freedom School to express this feeling and to attract the students; we read jealously the reports of other Freedom Schools in the cities, where it is much easier and where students are much more deeply involved as well as being more literate: Hattiesburg, 600 students, desperate shortage of teachers, ten more New York school teachers coming specially; Gulfport, 250 students; Moss Point, 200 students; Vicksburg, 300 students; McComb, 75 students on the lawn in front of the second church bombed in two days, while the young children play in the ruins. Everywhere there is enthusiasm, and everywhere students—on vacation—had eagerly awaited the Freedom Schools to end their boredom. Everywhere, that is, except Shaw . . .

The Freedom School coordinator in Shaw wrote to the state-wide director, Staughton Lynd.

Dear Staughton, Shaw, July 11

I think I am rapidly losing whatever effectiveness I may have had as a coordinator, or even as a rights worker. Part of it is family trouble. Virtually all letters and calls from my wife are depressing. She is frightened and also very concerned about our little boy who is lonely and quite upset by my absence. Because of this, I have in the last two or three days found it difficult to concentrate on my job here.

I could probably straighten this problem out and remain here, if it were not from something else even more important. I realize things are bad with us here because all we have been able to do is to fix up the school and community center and attend a few mass meetings. But during this time the depressing reality that surrounds me has been gnawing at my emotions until now I am completely frustrated. Living conditions here are so terrible, the Negroes are so completely oppressed, so completely without hope, that I want to change it all NOW. I mean this as sincerely as I can. Running a freedom school is an absurd waste of time. I don't want to sit around in a classroom; I want to go out and throw a few office buildings, not to injure people but to shake them up, destroy their stolen property, convince them we mean business . . . I really can't stand it here . . .

Wally

Staughton Lynd came to Shaw three days later. He and the coordinator had a long talk that night; the volunteers discussed their problem the next day, July 15.

July 16

The answer to our questions came as a result of voter registration work. We held a Freedom Day today at the courthouse of Bolivar county at Cleveland. We brought some 40 Negroes down to register, and 25 were allowed to take the test, an incredible success, and perhaps a record for any courthouse registration ever in Mississippi. For the younger people we held a picket line complete with freedom songs . . . Yesterday we had prepared the students for the picketing by special workshops in non-violence and picketing discipline. They had enjoyed them because they understood and valued the end to which we were directing them, and ever since they have been begging to go picketing again. It suddenly became clear to us that what we should do was to have special tutoring in anything the students desired.

Now we have something the students want, and over a third of the high school students—about 35—are coming here in the afternoon. Not only are they having special workshops in leadership and non-violence, but we are sneaking in all kinds of citizenship education, and they are enjoying it. We even have several who are interested in straight Negro history, and not too few who want academics, the normal type. So to this more limited, but under the circumstances healthier extent, we are underway as a Freedom School, the last in the state to do so.

Classes in voter registration work and political play-acting were a success everywhere. With innate sophistication about their own plight, the kids pretended to be a Congressional Committee discussing the pro's and con's of a bill to raise Negro wages, and "the con's" would discover neat parliamentary tricks for tabling it. Or they'd act out Senator Stennis and his wife having cocktails with Senator and Mrs. Eastland, all talking about their "uppity niggers." Sometimes they played white cops at the courthouse, clobbering applicants with rolled-up newspapers. . . .

Hattiesburg, July 24

We had a marvelous time at school today with a mock demonstration as a role-playing device designed to illustrate what Negroes have done to fight for their rights. A Volkswagen bus served as a "white only" restaurant complete with sign. The younger children, carrying and wearing signs, picketed in an orderly and very professional way, first in silence and then singing, according to the directions of their leader. They even held firm when at one point "a segregationist" poured water on them as they went by from a jug held over their heads. Along with some of the older girls, who played members of the Citizens Council, the white teachers played segregationists. This was a sort of test for both children and teachers: it took courage for us to assume this role and know the children might become frightened and more unsure than they are already of our real feelings, and it took courage for the children to accept our position as temporary. It ap-

102

peared that we all passed. The police, played with a vengeance by some of the older boys, came and hauled the pickets off to jail when they refused to disperse. The whole thing went off beautifully, with enthusiasm and spontaneous creativity displayed on all sides. Tomorrow we will hold a trial (something for which I am well prepared). . . .

Hattiesburg, Aug. 1

We have an 11-year old girl named Rita Mae who is the equal of the best of us. At one role-playing session, when I took the part of a Negro unwilling to register, I found myself unable to hold up the argument in the face of Rita Mae's logic, common sense, and determination. I could find no good reason why I should not register, and was ashamed to admit that I was scared, so I tried a dirty trick: I promised to go down, but said I needed a ride to the courthouse. This Rita Mae said she would provide; but when she came around with a friend in a car, I had skipped out and couldn't be found. Rita Mae ruefully admitted that the dramatization had a most realistic ending . . .

Hattiesburg, August 7

Today I went to Palmer's Crossing—a rural community outside Hattiesburg. There is a community center there and 2 Freedom schools. The student we talked to was a slim pretty girl who looked as if she'd just stepped out of the library at Willamette University where she'd graduated. Now she's living in a house where 4 families share a pump and an outhouse. She's a music major but her specialty here is literacy. She teaches individually at night and also has passed on to 6 high school students the literacy technics [the Laubach "Each one teach one" method] she learned at Oxford. Some of her students are over 75.

The Center was decorated from a teenage dance the night before for 135 youngsters. They called it "Swinging into Freedom" and had decorated with black and white hands of welcome on the front door. The two Freedom Schools were having a debate on the church lawn. *Resolved:* that violence is necessary to obtain civil rights. The points are outlined below. (The debaters were 12-16 years old.)

Affirmative:
1. It's too late for non-violence. (NV can only work if it can reach the conscience (eg. Gandhi and the British). The white

conscience is dead. The Jews practiced NV against the Nazis and were exterminated.

2. Violence has been successful in Africa—we must show the white man we aren't afraid. Haiti got freedom by violence—Joseph Saint led slaves to freedom after a revolt.

3. Violence shows people you aren't happy even if you don't win.

Negative:

1. Negroes should not stoop as low as whites.

2. We're out-numbered—life is a very precious thing—we can save lives by NV.

3. Love creates community between brother and sister.

4. Negroes have come a long way through NV (e.g. the Civil Rights Bill.)

Rebuttal Negative: White man's conscience isn't dead—I don't believe it and neither do you. Frederick Douglass may have fought but he fought harder with words. U.S. isn't 100% against us or how would Civil Rights Bill have passed?

Rebuttal Affirmative: People are afraid to use Civil Rights Bill—if you really believed it, you'd all enroll at Hattiesburg High (white). (This caused shouts of laughter.) People pick on you if you're NV—what good did it do Medgar Evers?

I regret to say the Affirmative won. The debaters were older and spoke better. Then there was the most spine-tingling singing of Freedom songs, led by a 15-year old girl who had been in jail several times. Every time a car with a white face passed, the children sang louder and waved. The cars slowed down but all summer no one has ever waved back. "Maybe someday they will," the children say . . .

Interaction between the classroom and life, education and politics came to a climax at the Freedom School Convention in Meridian on August 7-9.

Dear Mom, Dad, and kids . . .   Biloxi, August 16

The purpose of the convention was to formulate a youth platform for the Freedom Democratic Party, and the kids did a fantastic job of it. Each school sent three student representatives—about 120 in all—and a coordinator. There were eight different committees, each concerning a different area of legislation: jobs, schools, federal aid, foreign affairs, voting, housing, public accommodations, health. Sometimes the committee discussions were long and even bitter, particularly on foreign aid where a demand to boycott Cuba and all countries that trade with Cuba was adopted but then finally voted out in the general session. Resolutions in favor of land reform were voted down because they were considered too socialistic, but there is a history of Negroes' land being taken away from them here that was the basis of these vetoes. The kids really learned something from the convention; for the first time, Negro students from all over the state came together to discuss their common aims . . .

Love to all,
Al

White Mississippians didn't like the Freedom Schools any better than the rest of the Summer Project. It wouldn't have made any difference if the schools had offered only typing classes; the whole idea was dangerous. So they threatened parents who let their children go and they harassed the teachers and sometimes they destroyed the schools.

In rural Madison County, at a settlement called Gluckstadt, the Freedom School had been set up in a church known as Mt. Pleasant Society Hall. It opened later than most, but went very well . . .

Monday, July 20. The first day of school—14 students, ages 12 to 47. A student was assigned to report on civil rights news for the next few days . . . We gathered on benches under the trees. I asked one of the students to read an excerpt from a speech by Frederick Douglass. Asked three others to read aloud poems by Langston Hughes. When we finished, Arthur asked if he could take the Langston Hughes book home overnight.

Tuesday, July 21. Six students took turns standing and reading a play called "Protest," about a Japanese family confronted with change in the form of an alien, a chair. They seemed to enjoy it and three of them were quite good. Several of the boys went off by themselves and read Hughes' poetry aloud. I spoke to Mrs. —— about the possibility of building book shelves so the building could be used as a permanent library for the community (a library that could be increased by books solicited after I go home). I asked if she would be willing to act as librarian. She said she would think it over.

Wednesday, July 22. Discussed origin of slavery in America

—slave revolts—Negroes in the American Revolution—mutiny on the *Amistad*. It would be fine if we had a Pictorial History of The Negro for every student—less lecturing and more discussion. Two students and I read 3 of James Thurber's *Fables For Our Time*. Well received. Summaries written. Books signed out. Mrs. —— said she would act as librarian if we could get permission to use the building.

Thursday, July 23. Reviewed some myths about Negroes, asking students to give reasons why each was false. Some tried to defend them! Indoctrination has been well done . . . Walter reported on "The Harlem Rent Strike"—without using notes. Summaries of the day's work or essays on any subject were written.

Friday, July 24. 'Lectured' on the Reconstruction period. Discussed the Civil Rights Act of 1875. The big hit of the week was the poetry of Langston Hughes. There was hardly a time during the day when some one wasn't reading our one copy of *Selected Poems*.

Sunday, July 26. At church today the congregation agreed to have the library. Everyone seemed pleased at the idea because there has never been any library available to the Negroes here.

So it went for another week. More plans for the library. Poetry, plays, oral reports, written reports, study of political and power structure of Mississippi, classes in typing, Spanish, French, Drawing, History. Students driving *themselves* on in a hot, faded wooden building. "I didn't do so good on that report (an oral report). Could you give me another one?" (Ernest, age 18)

Tuesday, August 11. Gluckstadt Freedom School burned to the ground late last night. There is little doubt of the cause of the fire. There have been too many others like it in Mississippi. We start tomorrow to raise money to rebuild the building.

Complementing the Freedom Schools were the Community Centers which aimed to provide recreation and sports facilities, arts, handicrafts and libraries for a people who had little or nothing like that in their lives. They also offered sewing classes and sometimes a teen-age dance—but above all books, books, books . . .

I was overwhelmed at the idea of setting up a library all by myself. I had memorized the history of printing last summer session for the final exam, yet I did not know what the basic steps were for setting up a library and what the minimum essentials were. Then can you imagine how I felt when at Oxford, while I was learning how to drop on the ground to protect my face, my ears, and my breasts, I was asked to *coordinate* the libraries in the entire project's community centers. I wanted to cry "HELP" in a number of ways. . . .

We've done a lot of sorting of the 20,000 books that were dumped in our nice little community center, filling all the rooms. The temperature in those upstairs rooms was 110° . . . We've spent three days working to get to the windows. We sorted the books in the broken boxes (about 5,000), took the others to an old deserted house (the key to the house was immediately lost). Now I'm sorting the books on the newly built shelves into subject categories. . . .

Dear Mom and Dad,   Hattiesburg, Aug. 7

Nancy is now a full-time librarian, which she enjoys very much. She keeps the library open 8 hours a day (9-12, 3-6, 7:30-9:30) and it's very heavily used. She already has a thick file of names of borrowers. We have about 6,000 books in the library, main branch, and are opening new branches in several places in town and at Palmer's. (The Negro library supplied by the city has about 2,000 books or so. Negroes can also use books in the main library downtown but can't get a card or take anything out). What will happen to these libraries after we leave, heavens knows; finding people to continue the programs is number one problem now . . .

Love,
Joe

The most unusual Community Center of the summer was the one built in Mileston by a white man from California, who raised $10,000 for it himself and did much of the actual construction work. But the center in Harmony, a small rural community in Leake County, had its own special history; it was one case where getting the local people to assume responsibility for their center presented no problem.

The story began when the Freedom School teachers ran into difficulties shortly after their arrival . . .

Dear parents and sister and dog-sister, Carthage, July 1

. . . We are not actually in Carthage—that's a hot box. About 12 miles away is Harmony (pronounce Hominy), a Negro farm community of about 300-400 population. The people have been active for a long time in the NAACP. They were the first in Mississippi to file suit for integration of schools and consequently there was terrorism last year. Their hero is Medgar Evers, with whom they had a close relationship. Although few of the people have had much education themselves, they know the value of it. They speak intelligently and articulately. The first time I began to get excited and optimistic about our task here was when we arrived in Harmony. There was a welcoming committee of about 40 people out at the school to greet us. We didn't arrive until near noon, but the people had been there waiting since eight. All kinds of speeches were made to tell us how much we were welcome. It was great.

We are on a farm—180 acres—very prosperous by Mississippi standards . . . The farm is the most beautiful you could imagine—red, red dirt. Pines and other trees, hills, birds galore. The mockingbirds just won't shut up. To show how much of a country place this is, here is this morning's menu (breakfast at 7:00):

homemade biscuits
homemade jelly and syrup
fried eggs and bacon
grits
coffee with chicory
fresh milk (i.e., straight from the cow.)

They hardly buy any food—even their lard is home made. Choctaw Indians are all over. The women all wear long ruffled dresses with long sleeves and have aprons and sunbonnets. Hair down to their legs. Choctaws are pretty much classed with Negroes, who have a good feeling for them—a feeling of kinship. All Choctaws live on the reservation controlled by the federal government. There is some question as to their status under the civil rights bill. Seems to me they are included except that their school will not be integrated, as I now understand it. Why not?

We have four old school buildings—run down, wooden frame, few windows left—filthy. They are old for one reason. There has been no school for Harmony since 1961 [when the schools for the area were consolidated elsewhere]. But the people had entirely cleaned out one building, put in home-made chairs and tables and arranged the library—there are probably over a thousand books already. Today we worked cleaning out what will be our building. . . .

Love,
Judy

July 1

. . . About 20 adults, teens and young kids began to come to help clean out this gigantic school house, abandoned for over 6 years. The dust in each was inches thick; books were ripped in shreds and all over the floors and closets; loose glass was everywhere. It was a miracle—just like in *Lilies of the Field*. We sorted good and usable books from others, knocked all the loose glass out of the windows, 3 & 4 year olds were sweeping out rooms and carrying books to a huge fire where we were burning all the trash. In less than two hours, we were even pouring water over the floors and scrubbing them clean.

Then the sheriff came with about six white men, who were introduced as the "Board of Education." If they weren't Klan men, then they were at least Citizens Council people. God, they hated us. After we had finished cleaning the school, they told us we should not use it; it is county property. We told them it is private property [it did belong to the Negroes once but apparently had been deeded over later under complicated circumstances]. We are getting a lawyer and will fight in court. Meanwhile, tomorrow, Thursday, we will teach in a nearby church and outside. I fear that they will burn the school, and our library of 2 encyclopedias, *hundreds* of textbooks and actually *thousands* of hard-and-soft-covered books, donated from all across the U.S.A. . . .

The case was lost. Grass-roots enterprise went into action.

July 29

Everyday this week—the 22nd to 29th—the men of the community hammered and poured cement. At noon, about 7 or 8 women all gathered at the center with fried chicken, fish, salad, gallons of Kool-Aid and apple turnovers, and served them to the men, we teachers, and each other. It is a thing of beauty to see us all work together. Tuesday and Wednesday was the laying of the sub-floor. Two men cut the wood, two or three teenage boys and girls lay the wood down and ham-

mered it in, a few more are bringing more wood. We are a
living repudiation of the "too many cooks" theory. It should
be up by Saturday, or at latest Tuesday. The land was given
by a local man for "the sum of one dollar," and deeds were
drawn up. The teenagers are selling refreshments to raise
money for the center, as well as membership cards for a
dollar. It will hold the library, a snackbar, office space and
recreation area. . . .

August 6

The men (and some of us when we have time) work on
the building up to 10 hours a day with a 100° sun beating
down and the humidity so high one's clothing becomes soaking
wet after only a few minutes work. The building is guarded
at night because these people, after having had their homes
shot into and having a couple of crosses burned in the middle
of their community during the last few months, do not intend
to have all their hard work go up in flames right away. . . . .

August 5

About 4 men or teenagers armed with rifles and pistols
stand guard. Every local car that goes by has to honk a specific number of times . . . If anyone *does* attempt to bomb or
burn the center, they haven't got a *chance*. I live only about
50 yards away so I take over coffee, cookies, cigarettes,
tobacco, etc., to the guards and talk with them. . . .

*It was finished: a 30- by 60-foot frame building open to all
residents and supervised by a board of elected trustees. The
roof was barely up when Harmony began moving again on the
school situation.*

Aug. 10

The decision came Saturday night at a meeting in the
Galilee church. The day before the Carthage newspaper came
out with the shocking news: the 3 Negro schools of Leake
County are opening on Monday, August 10th, three full weeks
before the white schools. The reasons:

1) This was an attempt to stop the Freedom Schools two
weeks early.
2) They wish to start the Negroes early so that when they
pull them out of school in October to pick the white man's
cotton they can claim the Negroes can "afford" the time.

3) August 30th marks the 1st day of white registration. Due to a Federal court order the first grade is to be integrated. But if a first grader has already enrolled in a Negro school (and they'd have to do so if they went 3 weeks early), he cannot transfer. Therefore the idiocy was mainly to prevent school integration.

The parents and students of Harmony were really riled up and voted to boycott totally and use this as a "strike" for demands: equal student-teacher ratio, heat in the winter, better buses, no firing of Negro teachers for registering to vote, no hand-me-down desks, books and buses from the whites, etc.

And so today, the kids didn't go to school. It began pretty well—I'm told over half were absent. . . .

We spent three hours in Freedom School with all the children, ages 4 through 19. It was exciting and wild—we had the older teenagers each take two or three 2nd and 3rd graders and explain to them why we are boycotting. It was a joy to hear the youngsters work with each other. . . .

Later that month, Leake County schools were integrated after all. One Negro first-grader registered in the white school: a girl. But whether Mississippi rejected or accepted black children seemed less important at this point in history than what had happened to the children themselves.

Canton, Aug. 30

We were sitting on the steps at dusk, watching the landscape and the sun folding into the flat country, with the backboard of the basketball net that is now netless sticking up into the sunset at a crazy angle. Cotton harvesters went by—and the sheriff—and then a 6-year old Negro girl with a stick and a dog, kicking up as much dust as she could with her bare feet. As she went by, we could hear her humming to herself "We shall overcome" . . .

Mississippi is really two countries—
Negro Mississippi and white Mississippi,
and the difference is startling . . .

5 / The Other Country

THE KLAN LEDGER

An Official Publication of the White Knights of the
Ku Klux Klan of Mississippi (July, 1964)

We are now in the midst of the "long, hot summer" of agitation which was promised to the Innocent People of Mississippi by the savage blacks and their community masters. . . .

The recent events in Neshoba County and Statewide call for a message to the general public and the citizens of the great State of Mississippi. The arch-traitor and long-time betrayer of patriots the world over, Dulles, has used his lying tongue to try and convince the American public that this organization was involved in the so-called "disappearance". We were *NOT* involved, and there was *NO DISAPPEARANCE.* Anyone who is so simple that he cannot recognize a communist hoax which is as plain as the one they pulled on Kennedy in Dallas (and which Earl Warren is working so hard to cover-up), had better do a little reading in J. Edgar Hoover's primer on communism, "MASTERS OF DECEIT" . . .

There is no racial problem here in this state. Our system of strict segregation permits the two races to live in close proximity and harmony with each other and eliminates any racial problem . . . Bi-racial groups are the greatest danger we face in this State today. These groups have absolutely no legal standing whatsoever . . . Bi-racial groups have brought violence and bloodshed to every area in which they have been recognized. The surest way to have violence in Mississippi is for anyone to give any weight or recognize the authority of a bi-racial group. . . .

We are not going to recognize the authority of any bi-racial group, NOR THE AUTHORITY OF ANY PUBLIC OFFICIAL WHO ENTERS INTO ANY AGREEMENT WITH

113

ANY SUCH SOVIET ORGANIZATION. We Knights are working day and night to preserve Law and Order here in Mississippi, in the only way that it can be preserved; by strict segregation of the races, and the control of the social structure in the hands of the Christian, Anglo-Saxon White men, the only race on earth that can build and maintain just and stable governments. We are deadly serious about this business. We have taken no action as yet against the enemies of our State, our Nation and our Civilization, but we are not going to sit back and permit our rights and the rights of our posterity to be negotiated away by a group composed of atheistic priests, brain-washed black savages, and mongrelized money-worshippers, meeting with some stupid or cowardly politician. Take heed, atheists and mongrels, we will not travel your path to Leninist Hall, but we will buy *YOU* a ticket to the Eternal if you insist. Take your choice, *SEGREGATION, TRANQUILITY AND JUSTICE, OR BI-RACISM, CHAOS AND DEATH....*

Moss Point, Monday, July 6

Tonight the sickness struck. At our mass meeting as we were singing "We Shall Overcome" a girl was shot in the side and in the chest. We fell to the floor in deathly fear; but soon we recovered and began moving out of the hall to see what had happened . . . When I went out I saw a woman lying on the ground clutching her stomach. She was so still and looked like a statue with a tranquil smile on her face. I ran to call an ambulance and police . . .

It seemed as though a signal had been given. Two days later, the Project headquarters in McComb was bombed. On Friday, a Molotov cocktail was thrown at the Freedom House in Canton; in Hattiesburg a visiting Rabbi and two volunteers were severely beaten. On Saturday night, the Shaw project workers learned of a bombing plot as whites surrounded their office. The next day in beautiful old Natchez, a Baptist and a Methodist church were destroyed by fire—two of five Negro churches burned to the ground that week.

The week of July 6 showed that while there were relatively "good" and "bad" areas, violence could explode anywhere. Natchez and McComb had always been trouble, and there was originally some debate as to whether volunteers should go there at all. Eventually a few Negro and white male volunteers went to McComb, but no white women until the summer was over. Hattiesburg and Moss Point on the other hand were

*considered fairly peaceable. But in the end they all added up,
as the song says, to Mississippi Goddam.*

Each of the incidents had something to teach the volunteers about the attitude of Mississippi police and the pattern of law enforcement. In Moss Point, on the Gulf Coast, the victim was a local Negro girl of 17, Jessie Mae Stallworth. The occasion was a voter registration rally.

Moss Point, July 9

On Monday night we had a mass meeting, and the fifth district director, Lawrence Guyot, gave a terrific speech. The gist of his speech was that people say Moss Point is an easy area, "we have nice white folks here," that everyone has what they want already. But we don't have such nice white folks here, he said, and even if we did it shouldn't make us apathetic, it should make us want to take advantage of that extra little space . . . He kept saying, "What will it take to make you people move? A rape? A shooting? A murder? What will it take?"

At the very end of the meeting we were singing the last verse of "We Shall Overcome," 300 people in a huge circle. Suddenly there were gunshots, and all these people including me, hit the floor in a wave . . . A few seconds later we all got up trembling. A car of whites had gone by on the road outside and fired three shots through the open door. One Negro girl was hit in the side. She is in the hospital and is going to be all right, but nobody knew that at the time. The whole thing was additionally frightening because during the confusion when everybody was taking cover under tables etc., a piece of wire or something got caught in an electric fan and made a noise like a machine gun.

All during the meeting, the deputy sheriff was sitting there and the police patrol outside. The sheriff left shortly before the meeting was over and with him the police protection. At the time of the shooting there were no police anywhere around. Instead, they came fifteen minutes later, long after the whites had gotten away. . . .

. . . The boy who had been standing next to her, just outside the door of the meeting hall, said that there were four white men in the car. Kids were walking around saying, "They can't do that to us any more." It was only with much persuasion on the part of some of their friends and the COFO workers that they calmed down a little and went home. That night, the police arrested five Negro men. No white men!

115

These five had gone home for their guns and gone out to see if they could find the car from the description given. They saw what they thought to be the car. Some men in the car apparently fired at the Negroes. The five stopped at a gas station to tell some policemen what had happened. The police searched them, arrested them on charges of carrying "concealed weapons" and never followed the suspicious car. . . .

On the night of July 8, the pleasant-looking white frame home rented by the McComb project to serve as a "Freedom House" (living quarters and, in this case, the office too) shook to its foundations as a bomb sailed through a large picture window. The blast wrecked the wall and should have killed project director Curtis Hayes who was sleeping in that room—yet only two workers in all were injured, and only slightly at that. Like the Molotov cocktail which was served to the Freedom House in Canton two days later and failed to go off, it was one of several apparent miracles of the summer.

In the late morning of July 10, three white men and two Negro girls were returning from a morning of canvassing for voter registration in a Negro section of Hattiesburg. The men in the group were two white volunteers named Larry and Dave, and Rabbi Arthur Lelyveld, 51, a prominent reform rabbi from Cleveland, Ohio, who was with the Ministers' Project. One of the girls, Margie, was a volunteer, the other a local resident, Janet Crosby. They were on their way to the Morningstar Baptist Church, one of six churches in Hattiesburg where Negro women of the community served the usual big noonday meal to voter registration workers and Freedom School teachers.

Hattiesburg, July 10

I was writing a letter Friday morning about 11:45 when someone ran in saying that Dave was hurt. I and several others hurried back to the house behind the church to see what had happened. There was a small crowd on the patio and two people covered with blood. Dave was half-sitting, half-leaning on the back stoop, blood running down his chest, arm and back from a wound on the back of his head which the ladies were tending. The Rabbi was sitting on a wrought iron bench while the ladies tried to stem the flow of blood from a cut behind the right ear and a wicked gash over his right eye. Larry was helping, although I noticed he was favoring his arm. The two Negro girls were also there, neither was hurt. A car was commandeered to take the men to the

116

hospital . . . the kids dispersed and Margie told what she had seen and gradually began to regain control of herself.

They were walking along the railroad tracks. A white pickup truck stopped and two white men in it began shouting insults and profanities; the team walked on. Then the men got out and ran up the incline to the tracks in front of the five workers. The old man hit Dave who fell. . . .

Dave and then Larry continue the story:

. . . When I saw them swing, my thought was to use the old Karate, for it wouldn't have been hard. But nobody else would have helped me, so I didn't feel I could go against the Movement. The rabbi was hit on the first blow, I on the second. I fell to the ground, dazed but conscious, pulled my knees to my stomach, my hands covering my back, as we had been taught at Oxford. The rabbi stayed standing and took a number of blows. Larry was kicked. . . .

. . . The younger man with the iron rod started beating me about the head and shoulders . . . he struck me, pushing me over the tracks and down the embankment on the other side into a little ravine. He followed and kicked me with his work boots and beat me with his fists. He was swearing at me, calling me such things as "nigger lover," "white nigger" and "Commie," "Jew" and different combinations of these . . . At one point he grabbed up a handful of canvassing papers which had fallen down with me to the bottom of the ravine and tried to force them in my mouth. He then continued to kick me and beat me with his fists but as I had assumed the position I was able to ward off and soften the blows he gave me. When he finished beating me he said, "Run, nigger" . . .

Meantime the older man had been beating the Rabbi and he fell to the ground. The Rabbi had not remembered what he had been taught in orientation or else had not had any orientation as he did not know how to protect his head and abdomen from the blows . . .

The two Negro girls were not attacked at all. At one point, as one of them was kneeling over Dave to protect him as we had been taught in orientation, the white man looked at her and said, "I ought to wup you nigger" and then went back to beating the Rabbi.

. . . As I returned to the top of the bank the Rabbi was kneeling and blood was streaming from his head [the men had gone back to their truck by now]. I helped him to his feet and the five of us moved on down the track trying to get to

117

the church or into the Negro community where we would find safety and medical help. As we came to the first street which crossed the tracks, the truck—which we were no longer watching—came up behind us and attempted to run us down. We quickly stepped aside so as to put a small drainage ditch between ourselves and the truck. The truck stopped. The younger man leaped from the cab with the iron bar and said, "I'm goin' to wup 'em again". . . . I stepped beside the Rabbi . . . and said, "Haven't you hurt him enough?" The man . . . raised his weapon and hit the Rabbi again. I shielded the blow with my left forearm. This is where I incurred my major injury. The man then returned to the cab of the pick-up truck and they sat. We crossed the street heading toward the church as quickly as we could. I was holding the Rabbi as he was growing weak from the loss of blood. When we reached the corner, the truck sped up and came abreast with us. They glared. . . .

Professor Pease from Stanford University, who is working with the Freedom School teachers, and staying with me, was at a Volkswagen repair shop in Hattiesburg when the news came over the radio. He said the five white mechanics in the shop let out a cheer.

Dave had seven stitches taken in his head; Larry was treated for a fractured arm bone.

The day after the beating, Dave wrote:

We walked downtown to see the police this morning. The white people stared at us, and someone yelled from a passing truck, "what happened to your head, buddy?" All yesterday I couldn't believe that they really meant to hit us as hard as they could with those rods. Apparently they never were bothered by the thought that we were human and had feelings. I couldn't understand yesterday when the first one came swinging at us. . . . But somehow I understood after those stares we got downtown and the shout from the car.

Downtown we met a Negro girl in the movement. Yesterday the stares wouldn't have bothered me, but today they did. I just wanted to get away from her. I can now understand much better the feelings of those who have worked long in Mississippi. And I can see why they have ulcers. You just can never know when it's going to come.

And a week later . . .

118

One man has been arrested on the charge of assault with intent to maim in connection with our beating. I'm not at all sure what the chances are that a Hattiesburg jury will convict him, but it could be interesting. I'm sure that the FBI did the work, not the local police. The local police have asked me for no information except my name, age and address . . .

Almost a month after the beating, a grand jury hearing took place—supposedly to indict the man who had been positively identified by all four in the group. Larry continues the story . . .

Hattiesburg, August 7

. . . Then began a four hour game of musical chairs—a game so ironic and destructive, so tragic that a shame such as I have never felt came over me. We watched whites come in and out, shifting, moving chairs, and standing in order to avoid sitting next to a Negro. Chairs were moved from their places so that they partially obstructed the elevator door and one stairway. . . .

The first of our party, the Rabbi, was called into the Grand Jury Room. He was asked to tell where he had slept in Hattiesburg, whether Negroes and whites slept in the same room, whether there were any women of any color sleeping with them and how many beds, etc. The Rabbi asked that the relevancy of this line of questioning be explained to him so that he could answer the questions more completely. He was told that no one needed to "justify" any question put to him. . . . The last question put to him was whether we had been embracing the girls or in other physical contact with them preceding the beating. . . .

After an FBI official was interviewed, I was called, took the oath, and sat down. It was a long room dominated by a table and surrounded by a dozen red-faced men in open shirts and weathered necks and hands. I was asked the address of my family in Hattiesburg. At this time I asked if I could see counsel before answering that question and the interrogating District Attorney screamed, "NO!" He said, "Boy, you realize that you *may* be liable for contempt of these proceedings? Do you *refuse* to answer that question?" I replied politely that I would rather see counsel before I answered. Half standing he screamed, "Get outa this room," . . . his finger trembling. I left.

119

. . . We were required to wait until 3:00 P.M. before we were told to leave the waiting room. About two minutes before we were released, two lawyers from the COFO legal office appeared, consulted with us, and we all walked downstairs together. Within that interval, one of their brief cases was stolen. Later in an interview, the District Attorney made a slip of the tongue which indicated that he had read the contents of the case.

Since the hearing before the Grand Jury, we have found out that a semi-secret trial was held for Mr. Estus. He pleaded "no defense" in order to avoid having a public trial and our participation as witnesses. He was fined $500 and 90 days at hard labor—suspended. There was no newspaper coverage of the trial, the plea of no defense, or the decision.

The police in Hattiesburg had demonstrated only indifference when confronted by violence; the police in Shaw on the night of the bomb scare were—apparently—more concerned.

On Saturday, July 11, about 8:30 P.M., the Shaw project workers had gathered at the Community Center to relax a while from the 8 P.M. curfew they had been observing for security reasons. The project director, John Bradford, had go to the nearby town of Mound Bayou and was due to return soon.

Dear Mom and Dad,

. . . About 8:45 a Negro boy came to the door saying, "Tell Bradford not to come by the main road—there are men waiting for him."

Our reaction was slow. It was unreal; the night's heat and mosquitoes held our attention. We called Jackson, kept the line open and tried to contact Bradford.

At 9:00 a 20-year old Negro ran to the door talking in broken sentences—he had been offered $40 to tell where we were, and $400 to dynamite us. We frantically turned out the light, moved into one small back room—20 people and 100,000 mosquitoes—keep open line with Greenwood, call papers, local police, FBI, noises of cars passing and people outside—listening for bombs. Several people re-emphasizing their conviction that this summer is necessary and right, and glad they came down, regardless. . . .

Love,
Heather

The road had been blockaded with police, about forty of them. But the Project workers in the back room couldn't tell what was going on.

Mississippi has put everyone in a mild state of paranoia, but this is no imaginary situation. There are four cars at one end of the block. We're on the phone right now with the legal division in Jackson. They just informed us that we are not to leave the building, we'll be here all night—sleeping on the floor if we can sleep. . . .

. . . Well, we survived. The Sheriff came by this morning and told us he had put a guard around the whole Negro community last night. He was hurt that we called the FBI in. But he admitted that he should have told us about the guard. They never kept anybody away, anyway. Carloads of whites were driving by all evening until about 12:30. . . .

The sheriff told the newspaper that the bomb scare was a hoax of ours . . . But if it was a hoax, why waste forty guards on a Saturday night? And if he was really interested in protecting us, why hadn't he let us know what he was doing, instead of adding to our fear? The answer, in my mind, is that he wanted to scare us.

The volunteers' suspicion of the police was not unfounded. A lot of their activity was mere harassment: the police truck driving past a project office every 30 minutes with a German shepherd dog standing large and ominous in the back; the police cars circling at night, a spotlight turned suddenly in your face. Their favorite outdoor sport, however, was fining and arresting volunteers for traffic violations. The volunteers expected this and took care in most cases to get a Mississippi driver's license, Mississippi tags, and the inspection sticker which is necessary for a car after 30 days in the state. They kept their eyes glued to their speedometers and you could always tell a volunteer on the road because his would be the only car to come to a full halt before the big Mississippi STOP signs at railroad crossings—when there was no train in sight.

Batesville

The police gave us a hard time. All the time trumping up traffic violations. We were riding in a Volkswagen going 35 mph with the car in *third* gear. We were ticketed for going 110 mph. By-by $17. We are hard pressed for money.

121

Dear Mom and Dad,   Holly Springs, July 21

Harry and I went down to Canton to Harry's trial on a charge of blocking traffic with a truck load of books. A girl who is working in Canton also went to trial on a charge of running a stop sign on a corner where there is no stop sign. She paid a fine of $21 and Harry paid $23 . . .

The cops waited for Harry and me to leave town. As we were going north we saw two police cars pass us heading south. They were only a few minutes apart. Then about five minutes later two cars went around me and a cop came up behind. I had been careful not to go more than 55 mph in a 65 zone. The cop stopped me and said I had been going 75. When I told him I wasn't going that fast he got mad, took my driver's license and told me to follow him.

We went north to a gas station in Pickens where he called a judge to come hold trial . . . The cop said "Let me warn you about this judge, he's a real hanger. See that tree outside? He's hanged 15 guys from that tree. You can still see some little pieces of rope." He made several other remarks about hanging but it didn't scare us very much; we just looked at him.

He also asked what we thought of Goldwater. Harry is from New York. The cop said "Goldwater sure ran that nigger-loving Rockefeller crying back to New York, didn't he."

When the judge came in the cop pointed at me [a white] and said "This nigger here has broken the laws of the sovereign State of Mississippi." The judge didn't ask me to plead guilty or not guilty; he just asked if I had anything to say. I told him I was only going 55 and that two cars had passed me just before I was stopped. The cop said I was "passing everything on the road and was slowing down to 75 when I caught him." The judge said one of us was a liar, and that since he had known this policeman for a long time and since I was the first person ever to doubt his word, I must be wrong. So the fine was $27 or nine days in jail.

This wasn't enough though. When I had paid the fine I asked for my driver's license. The first cop told me the second cop had it. When I asked the second cop he said I had tried to run him off the road earlier that day. He told me to follow him back to Canton. When we got there I was charged with reckless driving and sent to jail on $100 bond . . .

Enough,
Larry

Occasionally an officer would come up with an original

charge, like "reckless walking" (on an empty road), or pro-
vide a bit of humor by asking the volunteer to write out the
ticket himself since "I don't spell too good." The police could
always pick up a person for "investigation," hold him up to
72 hours—which is legal in Mississippi unless a writ of habeas
corpus is obtained—and eventually confront him with an
offense.

Jackson

Three local high school students and myself were passing
out hand bills about Martin Luther King's visit the next day.
As we often would because of the hot sun, we stopped at a
small cafe for a soda. It was about four in the afternoon. Two
huge cops, noticing my car, came in. They fooled around for
about five minutes and then asked my three friends for identification. Then they told the three to go with them. Up to
then they hadn't said a word to me. I asked if the three were
under arrest. They said "yes." I asked on what charge. I was
then told to shut up or I'd be taken in also. The cops then
said the three were under arrest for "investigation."

After I had called the office to report the incident, I started
back. As soon as I turned onto the highway, a waiting police
car came in behind me. I was arrested for improper tags (I
had Wash. State tags), taken to the station, charged $29, and
put into jail because I didn't have it. The bail soon came and
I was out. But the other three, it turned out, had been charged
with being drunk. The jailer would not let the lawyer see
them. The cops refused to give them a drunk test. Finally, I
bailed them out at $15 apiece.

Next day we had a long trial. The three who were charged,
myself, and the boy who works in the cafe testified that all
four of us were drinking orange soda and had not had any
alcohol that day. Our lawyer made the cops look like fools
in the courtroom. When asked by the judge if they could
identify the three as the ones arrested, one said, with a wave
of arm, "Yeah, I think that's them three niggeresses over
there." The other cop said he was sure of one, but not of the
others. Finally, at the end, we were amazed at the verdict.
The judge could never reflect on the good character of the
officers, but dropped the charges because the cops didn't make
a positive identification of the three . . .

Law enforcement in Mississippi could become even more
amazing if you were being attacked by local whites and called
the police for help.

123

About a week after the Rabbi was beaten in Hattiesburg, a young volunteer in that town went to buy some poster board with two fellow workers . . .

Hattiesburg, July 21

There were three of us—Bill, a Negro, Peter, white and I [a white girl]. Realizing the risk of being in an integrated group, we first decided to split up, with Peter and me following Bill; but it was so awkward being unable to talk together, and so obvious that we were all together anyway, that we decided to abandon the arrangement. . . . We were walking three abreast, Peter closest to the curb, I in the middle. Bill entered the drugstore . . . Suddenly a man jumped Peter from behind. I was so astonished, I hardly grasped what was happening. Peter was knocked down and curled into the non-violent protective position against the building—the man was kicking him in a fury, but almost methodically and without a word.

All I could do, in accordance with "the rules" was try to get help, and should the beating go on too long, shield Peter's body with mine. I yelled "Help—police," loudly and clearly, over and over. Finally a policeman arrived and pulled the man off. (It seems he had been at the corner directing traffic and could have made it more quickly.) Another policeman quickly joined the first, who led the man away, and detained us when we started to follow—as if to let the two get out of sight so the man could quietly be released. We hurried after them anyway.

At the station house, Peter heard for the first time that *he* was under arrest, along with his assailant, for assault and battery. We all reacted indignantly and vociferously, demanding how that could be. The policeman said that whenever there was "fighting" in the street, both parties were arrested. We said that there had hardly been a fight . . .

Every brush with the police contained a reminder that the missing three had last been seen alive on their way to jail. There were ugly stories about what could happen to a man in the privacy of prison, in the hands of the law. But more commonly jail was just a nuisance for the volunteer.

Gulfport, July 8

We were booked and taken to a cell block on the second floor with about 8 white prisoners already in it. Standard procedure is to bribe some prisoners with cigarettes to beat up civil rights workers. However, we soon made friends and in ten minutes we were removed to an empty cell block on the third floor with women, juveniles, and condemned murderers. We sang freedom songs, beat rhythm on the bars and metal table, played kazoos of tissue and combs and raised hell.

The Harrison County jail is very modern, but you sweat, for Mississippi is a hot place. Jails are so damn stupid, though. Once you're in, and the lethargy and the apathy stick, you're stuck. The theory is deterring, but who is deterred? The theory is reform, but who reforms? You just sit, or sleep, or stare, or think about something, or dwell on nothing. Jail apathy very quickly becomes life to the inmate. But this apathy permeates everything only while you are in jail. When you are set free, it explodes in one big binge of rebellion. . . .

Kenneth Keating (R-NY) called through an aide about a half hour after our 9:00 breakfast the next day—Barry and Dave are his constituents. The sheriff came up personally to give us hell for not eating his food. We turned it down in protest against segregated jails, arrest under an unconstitutional law, and because we got better facilities outside—a dig at the sheriff. He cannot comprehend why we live with Negroes. It is so foreign and strange an idea that his mind just stops. We finally got out on $500 a piece property bond.

Unlike workers in the early days of the Movement, the volunteers usually didn't remain in jail more than overnight. But once in a while . . .

Panola County Jail
Dear Family,   Batesville, Friday ca. 1:30 P.M.

I am writing this letter as I begin my second day in jail, but bond is set at $700 and the trial for tomorrow at 10:00 A.M., and I have read the *Sat. Eve. Post. Life, Mad,* most of a Baptist publication called *Gospel Light,* 12 pages of a pulp western, odd bits of newspaper, and parts of *Car Life,* all very thoroughly, and am now at the end of my resources. Not stir-crazy—just restless. I'm well and alone in a large bunch of cells, tolerably clean and unmolested. I just had an amiable conversation with the sheriff. But I do wish someone would get me out of here. An attorney and a law student are in town, but they don't seem to have secured bail money yet. I'm in on two charges: failure to answer questions of the D.A. and resisting arrest . . .

125

I tore these pages out of the back of a Bible. But I'm furious—and anxious to communicate the fact. Who the hell do they think they are? At my trial, the Sheriff and a State Highway Patrolman, who was in mufti when I was arrested, testified that (1) the sheriff had told me I was under arrest (2) when grabbed by the arm by the Deputy, I had raised my arm to ward him off (3) I had held back after being grabbed. All of which are untrue. The point is, they never did make a proper arrest. Only the D.A.—no officer—told me I was under arrest; the others only said, "Let's go" and so on . . . The D.A. also asked me what organization I belong to, and I told him COFO, Spee Club, Hasty Pudding. I hope he does some research into that.

The very same State Highway Patrolman, back in mufti after dressing up for my trial, came around to my cell. Infuriating and frightening middleaged bastard. Parts of our conversation:

"They wash that nigger smell off you?"

"I'm sorry, sir, I don't understand."

"They give you a bath to get that nigger smell off you?"

"Well, I took a shower yesterday, sir."

"That oughta help."

And when I mentioned that I had a Bible in here: "Look it up where it says about mongrelizin' of black and white degeneratin' the races."

"What chapter and verse is that, sir?"

"I don't know, but it's in there."

"The Bible is a big book, sir. I can't find it if I don't know where to look."

"You don't *want* to find it, that's why."

Then he launched into an analogy about mangy mongrel dogs. I never got up the courage to ask him about the "mongrelization" already accomplished, of which there is ample evidence all around. Ah, but he knows all that . . . The trusty, who's a pretty likeable, apolitical, troubled alcoholic, assured me that in the past, Negroes had to be lynched, summarily "cause otherwise they'd run all over whites." It's a curious kind of reasoning, but of course it is the prevalent line of thought, world-wide.

We can't skirt the idea of Freedom and agree that first and foremost, the cops have to keep order, and *then* we can progress . . . Order! I guess things are pretty well ordered on the mechanical side for most Americans. But emotionally, imaginatively, intellectually . . . why can't people admit not only that they fear the chaos but that they *are* the chaos?

Later.

I can't sleep, though I've finished *Borstal Boy* and reread *Invisible Man* and *The Stranger,* attentively, and also some of yesterday's Memphis paper, and, by God, I hate this old world. To think that someone as egocentric and self-pitying and cowardly and self-righteous as myself could have some effective grasp on a simple concept of justice which evidently strikes most people as either treacherous or nonsensical or unimportant or too dangerous! Dangerous! Wow! What's dangerous is closing our eyes like we all do most of the time and hoping we'll never see the dangers. I do hope that when I'm old, and this struggle, if it *is* to be won, is won, all of us, and everyone we touch or even brush by, will live in a more gutsy, moment-to-moment, existential fashion, whether for love or for hate, for creation or for destruction. And perhaps love will come of all this. I'm not ashamed to use the word right now, for I feel very attached, very loyal to the common but infractable bits of passion and affection and desire and appreciation and enjoyment and loyalty that are what it comes down to, if one lives for any reason other than to keep from dying. Tell everyone I'm well and that if they want me to go back to Harvard in the approved style, they simply do not understand.

Monday

No action today from COFO, but the most active day yet for me inside the jail! The Deputy volunteered me the use of a razor after I asked and received permission to take a shower. Result: using a broken rearview mirror, my worst shave ever. After five days, what will you? Another result, the towels on which I wrote this. Furthermore, after the shower I had time to talk to the Negro prisoners in their cell . . . They gave me a whole bunch of Superman comics. I also read the Book of Amos *aloud.* I don't know if anyone listened enough to get the point.

But most exciting of all, two young, (late 20s—early 30s) respectable, white citizens were allowed back here by the deputy with the intention of engaging me in conversation, which they did. Since they were unofficial, I let myself go more than I did with the Highway Patrolman last night. Mostly the same old guff, although they seemed to believe me when I said that I wasn't a Communist. One of them owns and operates a 1500 acre plantation; I don't know what the other does. It's very hard to dig them—you know, both sides polite, furious and afraid and contemptuous of the other . . . The parting shot was revelatory. "You guys are all the same. Your ideas are all shallow and philosophical, not based on practical experience with people." The weird part was that both looked my age or younger, right down to hair style. It's a depressing country, and I don't mean Mississippi. I realized, talking to them, how much money-as-status must mean to the Citizens Council types.

Oh, God, I don't know what to do about my white brothers. All the assumptions, implicit or explicit, pragmatic or theoretical, of the "white-is-right-Anglo-Saxon-uber-alles" variety are part of what keeps me in this jail. That's not an unfair statement, even allowing for the personal responsibility of the Sheriff and the D.A. . . .

Just think of how I was raised! Private school, indeed. I suppose that's a bit sophomoric, but I think I'll want my children to go to some place like a city high school, where social snobbery isn't as tight, and knowledge of other social classes not so difficult to obtain . . . I'm still, au fond, a moralist. There's a lot of truth about all of us—y'all too—in Eric Hoffer's *The True Believer*.

Lies—the thing about someone like Mr. Jones. His family had a plantation . . . the system induced him not to *know* what the black folks thought and felt. Yet he's intelligent, he should at least have guessed sometime . . . but his fine intellect was never attached to the will to be critical enough of his own environment. If moralists won't analyze and criticize environments, it's all in the hands of B. F. Skinner and BBD & O.

As you and I have found, abstract support for "Civil Rights"—the newspapers and other outsiders call it Civil Rights and we call it *Freedom*—isn't worth much to the people who are catching hell. You've got to catch some of the hell yourself . . .

Tuesday

Out today at 1:00 P.M. on bond of $350 plus $100 = $450. Trial Saturday . . . Don't worry 'bout me. Back to my base today, I think. I hope you can read these jottings. I write from outside jail.

Yours in the struggle,
Morton

*Harassment, arrest, jail—the volunteers quickly learned
what to expect from the Mississippi police. Yet the pattern
had a certain complexity. Law enforcement varied from
county to county, partly because the sheriffs—elected officials
whose power could be hard for a Northern city-dweller to
imagine—ranged from peaceable men to notorious killers.*

Clarksdale, August 8

. . . Clarksdale, like so many other Southern towns, re-
mains somewhat autonomous from state government and the
local government is run by the police. Instead of a police
state, Mississippi is a conglomeration of police communities . . .

*In the courtroom, too, there was variation—at least on the
surface.*

Clarksdale

Before the trial began, we had packed the courtroom. A
policeman entered with a can of air deodorant, and sprayed
all of us who were in the room. Since most of us were Negro,
it was a subtle reminder that all Negroes are supposed to
smell bad. Most of us just chuckled.

Dear Mom and Dad,   Hattiesburg, July 21

At the hearing [for the volunteer who had been arrested
after being beaten] Peter was granted continuance until
Thursday, but the assailant, a Mr. Houston Hartfield, was
tried and we all had to testify as witnesses for the city. The
city prosecutor, oddly enough, has the same last name as
mine, and a daughter named Susan. He and the judge seemed
fairly reasonable; at least, though they are segregationists,
they couch their sentiments in polite phrases. The attorney
for the defense, on the other hand, was coarse, theatrical and
stupid. The judge continually reprimanded him for his method
of questioning . . . But the highlight of his performance
was when Bill innocently used the term "comrades" to mean
friends. He recoiled, then pounced on the word, weighted it
with insinuation . . . Then he stepped back, inflated himself,
and after an impressive pause, demanded ponderously, "Are
you now, or have you ever been . . ." It was quite ludicrous.
Bill asked the judge if he had to answer, and the judge wearily

gave an affirmative. In a completely candid and somewhat amazed fashion, Bill shrugged, "No" . . .

Later:

The judge said at the outset Thursday that it was with great pain that he was forced to render the verdict—that he and the entire community were in complete sympathy with Mr. Hartfield and would very likely have reacted in the same way to "the situation" (I assume he meant ourselves as a mixed and therefore noxious group). He declared that we were destroying everything accomplished in race relations here through gradualism and education. He could say this, before a segregated courtroom in a courthouse cluttered with white and colored signs, where Negroes are addressed by their first names and must submit to derogatory appellations. It was a lengthy sermon concluding with the warning that if any of us again appeared before the court it would be extremely difficult for whoever occupied the judge's bench to remain impartial.

Mr. Hartfield was pronounced guilty and fined $40 with $20 off on good behavior. The case against Peter was dismissed. We were given by the lawyers to understand that the decision, unimpressive as it may seem, was unusual. . . .

Love,
Susan

The one thing that no Mississippi authority wanted, from Senators Eastland and Stennis on down, was another invasion of federal officials and newsmen such as had occurred in Philadelphia. That event, as much as anything, made the Summer Project less bloody than everyone had expected. And so in some areas, it seemed as though the circling police cars really were there to protect the volunteers—at least from being killed . . .

Meridian

A member of the Citizens Council told me that the Meridian Citizens Council had voted in June to "ignore" the presence of COFO workers for the summer. The Meridian police are amazingly cooperative. But this decision to be patient is based on a belief that COFO would leave Mississippi with the sunflowers—and take all the radio and TV and newspaper men and the FBI with them ...

Shaw, July 7

Yesterday, the third day of our stay here, I was among four volunteers driven up by the local police chief to see the sheriff of the county. The sheriff . . . told us that every Mississippian's blood boiled, that he felt a physical revulsion when he saw us; but he would protect us to the hilt in order to protect the image of his beloved state of Mississippi and of his country ...

That was the "white power structure"; what about the people of Mississippi? Probably the large majority just looked at the volunteers—but in a very special way.

Gulfport, July 29

A while before I came down I read John Griffin's *Black Like Me* and he speaks of the hate stare . . . It's really the most terrifying and ugly thing imaginable. When it was first given to me I had a reaction that combined fear and shock. Fear because you realize the power that someone like that will use, and shock that the human face could be that way.

Meridian

. . . It's impossible to describe the type of stares one receives around here for walking or driving in an integrated group . . . Yesterday, there were two cars driving by the house where I'm staying and the first car slowed down . . . the second driver, watching us rather than the road, nearly smashed into his colleague ...

Vicksburg, July 10

. . . Since so many people drive slowly past and stare at us and sometimes even bring the family and park (like a drive-in movie), we've hit upon a plan to get free meals. Put up a sign:

C.O.F.O. ZOO   VISITORS WELCOME
Nonviolent Animals
PLEASE FEED

And the crank calls: sometimes a threat—"don't go to sleep tonight if you want to wake up tomorrow"—and sometimes just unflattering adjectives . . .

Dear Friends,   Meridian, July 20

Once again I find myself spending the night "guarding" the COFO office, a task which consists mainly of answering a more or less constantly ringing telephone only to be greeted by the voice of some well-wisher who employs the sort of language which it would probably be illegal to send through the mails. Often these people remain merely silent and hang up the receiver, but at times they become more daring and toss off witty remarks about our mothers and our morals. Every once in a while one of them forgets his script and has to be coached by whoever is sitting next to him at the time . . .

While I'm in a "lighter" mood (and you have to be in order not to get driven crazy by these callers), I'll note that the omniscient *Meridian Star* has been very instrumental in protecting us from any possible physical violence on the part of the local aristocrats. Besides calling us left-wing fanatics (which I might be . . . who knows?), race-mixers, trash, and a lot of other such things, they have continually gone into full descriptions of our physical appearance. Naturally, besides being dirty, long haired . . . and, in general looking like we just crawled out from under a trash can (that's their description, I'm not making it up), it seems that we all (I'm not sure if the girls are included) have beards. So far, I have yet to meet one person on the project with a beard (people were strongly urged to shave them off in Oxford).

The result is that, unless we're walking in integrated groups, it would be hard for the local citizenry to recognize us—they're all on the lookout for Christ figures or something.

Best,
Peter

Specialized harassment included the telephone company giving elaborate excuses for not installing service in a project office; the widespread tapping of project telephones; the bank's refusal to open an account; the nondelivery or delaying of mail; the inch-long tacks sprinkled across COFO driveways . . . These things, like the traffic tickets, were more irritating than fearsome—yet they suggested what lay below the surface.

Hello to all friends of freedom,   Carthage, July 23

Being unsure of what I actually said to Daddy, I want to tell you all everything I can remember about the incident.

Three other girls and myself went into Carthage today to shop, do laundry, and call home. All our business was done within an hour except my call home. Having been told that our old place from which we called was frequented by "two hoodlums whom the sheriff can't control," we chose a drive-in cafe which had two outdoor phone booths in the parking lot. I went in to make my call.

I guess Daddy and I had talked about five minutes when this redneck . . . came to the booth and asked me in a testing way through the half-open door if I would talk longer. I knew what he meant because of the empty booth next to me.

"I'll be through in a minute," I said.

"You'd better be through *now* and get out," was his response, delivered in a threatening tone.

Then Daddy asked me if that was Hank. I was momentarily puzzled as to what to do as I surveyed the situation. I was trapped in the phone booth with this character's foot in the door (my mistake to let that happen). I wasn't scared but just a little confused.

The best thing, I decided, was to frighten him away by describing him to Daddy on the phone.

"No, this is a strange man whom I've never seen before. He is about 5'6". He's wearing a cowboy hat . . ."

I think I slammed down the receiver on "hat" because as I began the sentence he waved an open pocket knife at me with his right hand. When he heard my description he glared and went around to the back of the phone booth. This startled me and for some reason I thought he could electrocute me; actually he would have been hurt himself because his intention, and he almost did it, was to cut the phone wire. The girls in the car had the door open and the motor running. . . .

At the junction with 488 we found two cars with three men in each waiting for us. Anne, luckily, was a good driver and had presence of mind. She whipped around the corner and got in front of the two cars. We had to go well over 80 mph to stay ahead of them (only one car chased us). They could have tried to run us off the road. We knew we would be safe once we got to our dirt roads. . . .

Love,
Judy

Dear family,

Saturday afternoon, several of us were invited out to a farm 6 miles from town for a day of picnicking, swimming, relaxation and V.R. work out in the country . . . Bill Haden, a white COFO worker from Oregon, a local Negro and myself were sitting along the edge of the lake about 400 yards from the farmhouse singing some songs and playing the guitar. Just after finishing the last verse of Dylan's "Who Killed Davy Moore," we saw two whites coming towards us down the path from the farmhouse. Since we were expecting other people from the COFO office to be joining us, we didn't think anything strange about this. When they got somewhat closer and I didn't recognize them, I asked Bill if he knew who they were. He didn't know. A few seconds later, the younger man (about 5 feet 10, 200 lbs.) came up to me and asked me if I knew Dixie." I told him, I wasn't sure, to which he responded, "Well, you'd better be sure, and quick." I told him, "Well, sit down. Maybe we could work it out together." He told me just to play it. I've never learned a song quite so fast in all my life.

Apparently, he didn't appreciate my efforts, because the next thing I know, the guitar was out of my hands, kicked, and thrown out into the lake. Almost simultaneously, about 15 other rednecks, about 25-55 yrs. in age, emerged from the trees and brush surrounding the lake. The other man, who had first come up, began beating me with the big wooden club. I saw that it would be impossible for me to run around the edge of the lake back to the house without being further attacked and beaten. So, since I was born for the water, home I went. After I was 15 or 25 feet out, he pulled a pistol from beneath his shirt and began firing in my direction. Ten or twelve of the other men began shooting in the direction of the house and the fleeing COFO worker with pistols, rifles and shotguns.

When the bullets began hitting the water, not five feet from my head, I thought it was time to make a submarine exit. Coming up about a hundred and fifty feet further out, the bullets were splattering even beyond me, perhaps 30-40 feet. Since I didn't see any men at the other end of the lake, I was hoping to swim there, get out, and try and make it to the house. About ten minutes later, as I got out of the lake, two men came towards me out of the brush. The man in front had a forked tire iron and the man behind him had a steel chain.

Since old freedom fighters never give up, I again tried to humanize with the cat, asking him "Wouldn't you like to sit down so we can talk this thing over? Although we might have our differences. . . ." While I was saying this, I was gradually taking a few steps back toward the lake, just in case he did not respond positively. Well, he didn't. Menacing the tire iron, he ordered me to get over to where the rest of the men were and not get wise. For a few more seconds, I tried to reason with him . . . Just about at that moment, one of them comes from the brush around the lake with his club. He swings it at me across the back and the man with the tire iron hits me across the knee while I think the man with the the chain hit me across the ribs and back. Deciding that it was better to be a live chicken than a dead duck, I got the hell out of there. By some miracle, I was able to make it through the brush, barbed wire and all the shooting (by now from both sides) up to the farmhouse.

When I arrived, the COFO office had already been notified and I got on the phone immediately to the FBI in Laurel. After about five minutes, an FBI agent called back and wanted to know what was going on. I told him that the Civil War was reoccurring and would he *please* come on out—with the rest of the Federal Gov't. He wanted to know if we had notified the local police and sheriff's office. I told him we had, but they refused to be of any assistance. I then asked him if he could not protect us, would he be so kind as to come out and take pictures down by the lake of the man who had been firing on us? We exchanged a few more words, and I went to lie down on the floor. I vaguely remember the sheriff arriving maybe a half hour or 40 minutes later and taking the names of everybody in the house. We asked him if he would give us protection back to Laurel or at least ride with us. He replied, "I didn't carry you trouble-makers out here and I'm sure not going to take you back." With this, he left us. About 15-20 minutes later, the ambulance arrived and we were taken to Jones County Community Hospital. . . .

That's all for now, take care, don't worry,

Love,
Dave

The symbol of unpredictable violence was the pick-up truck with gunrack and two-way radio, and no license plate (a single one for Mississippi) in many cases. Sometimes the driver removed the plate or covered it with a paper bag for his own sinister reasons. Sometimes he just didn't have one. You couldn't be sure.

The pick-up truck was the trademark of the redneck, the rural white—usually poor—who works all day in the open *and thus gets a sunburned neck. People call them crackers in Georgia, peckerwoods elsewhere. The volunteers dreaded the redneck above all other whites, and during the summer of 1964 they generally had more to fear from him than the police. But in many areas it seemed as though there was not much difference between the antennae on a man's truck and the one on the police car.*

In the small rural town of Marks, a carload of workers from Clarksdale went canvassing. . . .

Clarksdale, August 12

I was stopped and questioned by the City Marshall, the only police officer in Marks. On finding out who I was, he cussed me out and demanded repeatedly that I hit him—if I was any kind of man. He told me to get into the car; the charge was "suspicion" because there were many "bank robberies and car thefts in the area." I was taken to the Sheriff's office and interrogated. The Marshall said he would give me and my fellow civil rights workers no protection and in fact he was looking to "get us" and if he couldn't get us some of the townspeople would and he would be elsewhere when things were happening.

On the way back to where he picked me up, he stopped at two gas stations to show the folks what a "Communist civil rights worker bastard" looked like. Then I was released . . . Angry mobs of whites were gathering at street corners and it was getting late—a sure sign of possible trouble. Finally we got a group of Negroes to escort us home but at that moment "deputies" came and told us to get out of town. We had to leave unescorted on the main highway when we had planned on a more discreet route.

We started down the highway and we saw 3 or 4 cars parked ahead and 3 or 4 cars converging on that spot from a side road. We felt sure that it was some type of road block since it was about midnight and we hadn't seen people congregated on corners and we knew that the deputies and townspeople were in close contact. I turned the car around and headed in the other direction at breakneck speeds. . . .

And in Greenwood, this is what happened to a voter registration worker who was beaten but managed to get his attacker arrested that same day:

136

. . . At the police station the insidious relation between the local law officials and the local law-breakers grew more obvious. A police officer was playing with a knife, rubbing his thumb over its edge. He pointed the knife at a girl, a co-worker, and said that he kept it sharp for "niggers like you." He then pushed her around. My assailant, still present, started in on one of the white workers, accusing him of being a "nigger-lover," and suggested to the officer that he castrate the boy. A bit later, he and my assailant both drove a Negro boy home who had been in jail.

We finally started to leave the station late that night, but we couldn't because all four of our car tires had been slashed. The Negro boy who had been driven home by them later told us that as they passed our car, one said, "There's the car those bastards are driving." We have good reason to suspect that the law enforcer, and the attacker, slashed the tires.

The man who beat me is now free. He paid a $25 fine. He is a friend of the judge's, of the police, and a member of the Citizens' Council. It is amazing that he was even fined. He probably would not have been one month ago. Still, it is no comfort to me. He is free, he is angry. He knows that he can get away with much worse. The FBI would not arrest him . . . I have no local protection. I have no Federal protection . . .

Coming from lunch the other day to the COFO office we noticed a hush unusual for that place. A boy in a bloody shirt was reporting a brutal beating via phone to the FBI . . . The FBI will "investigate" and no more.

Where is the USA? It is a violation of FEDERAL LAW to harass voter registration workers. Where are the Federal Marshalls to protect these people? How do the Negroes defending "democracy" in Viet Nam feel about the defense that democracy gets in Mississippi?

On July 10, J. Edgar Hoover arrived in Jackson at President Johnson's request to open the first statewide F.B.I center since 1946. He announced that there were now 153 agents in the state; he also announced that they weren't there to protect civil rights workers.

The F.B.I. had the power to arrest when a violation of constitutional rights was taking place. They used that power once in Mississippi on June 26, when three voter registration

137

workers were threatened at Itta Bena. They used their arrest power once again, under the Civil Rights Act, in Greenwood.

Jackson, July 13

The FBI is acting a little more quickly—but only because of your pressure on the federal government. And they aren't much help because they're really not on our side. To investigate the bombing in Ruleville, they went around asking intimidating questions of the local Negroes. . . .

Dear friends, Ruleville, July 18

At around ten P.M., 14 F.B.I. agents came to interview us [a group of volunteers and staff workers jailed for "unlawful distribution of literature"]. The two staff workers were not enthused about talking with them . . . In the past they have sometimes turned statements over to the local officials, thus giving away the defendant's hand. This fear was confirmed the next day. One of the guys overheard the chief of police ask the FBI for our statements and the FBI man said, "Well, we'll talk about that later." I tried to get them to promise not to give my testimony to the police. They were evasive . . .

The next morning the F.B.I. came back to interview us. They were pretty square with me, but asked some of the others irrelevant questions about their past political activities . . .

Love,
Mike

A whole world had come crashing down; terms like "law and order" or "responsible Negro leadership" became meaningless. When, on July 16, Barry Goldwater was nominated at the Republican Convention in San Francisco and the first of the Northern city riots broke out in Harlem three days later, the volunteers had little patience with all the talk about white backlash. The Mississippi newspapers were exultant about both events.

Dear everybody, Bolivar County, July 28

. . . The Harlem riots have really been spread all over the newspapers down here. After living in a Negro community for a while it is a lot easier to see why riots occur . . . Nobody has to "agitate" Negroes to make them dissatisfied. All it takes is something to trigger it off . . .

Medgar Evers wrote that in his younger days he wanted to

138

start a guerrilla war in Mississippi. Some of the young people here have come close to advocating the same thing—"Some of the guys, they don't buy this nonviolent stuff. We want to get out and DO something." After facing a few bombings, beatings and jailings some of the summer volunteers felt like throwing a few bombs back themselves . . .

Yours for freedom,
Robert H.

Hattiesburg, August 12

. . . a brief comment on the note you scribbled across the article you sent me regarding the moratorium on demonstrations. "This is what I suggested to you in June needed to be done, and you disagreed at the time. Now the Goldwater threat is so great that certainly rioting must cease—at least for now."

I suppose you might call riots demonstrations—but the reverse is not true. Demonstrations are not riots. How dare you suggest, as you do in saying "rioting must cease—at least for now," that demonstrations and rioting alike originate from the Movement? Yes, of course, the rioting must cease, and not just for now, but for always. Have you thought about what positive steps might be taken to *prevent* it? . . .

The volunteers had learned only too well how "violence" depends on who does it. How a society can conspire against you. With no local protection and no federal protection, fear becomes the climate of life . . .

Ruleville

It's night. It's hot. No lights because there aren't any curtains—meaning they can see you and you can't see them. *They,* the word *they,* takes on its full meaning here. You slap at a dozen or so mosquitoes that are buzzing in. You doze off and the phone rings again, about the fifth time, and the other end stays mum. By now you know that somebody, someone on the other side, knows where you are. They know who you're staying with . . .

Violence hangs overhead like dead air—it hangs there and maybe it'll fall and maybe it won't. Sometimes it's directed at people in the movement, sometimes it's indiscriminate. Cars have been roaming around; seven or eight vigilante trucks with their gun racks and no license plates have been seen meeting at the city dump. What will they do? When? Something is in the air, something is going to happen, somewhere, sometime, to someone . . . A few nights ago cars roamed the streets, empty bottles flew from their hands, striking cars and homes. They were empty that night—the next night the bottles were loaded—exploding as they hit the church and setting it afire.

Canton

When any cars come here, Karol and I do a disappearing act into the back of the house. So far we've had no trouble. Sometimes around midnight when the dogs start barking we feel rather strange. Last Saturday night they started howling about 12:30 A.M. Karol and I turned out the lights and listened. The barking came closer and got louder until we heard footsteps under our window. The chase continued around the house while everybody else slept. Karol and I sat very still and listened. "I'd like to use the pot," Karol said, "but not with the Klan watching." The barking soon stopped and we fell asleep. Next morning, a neighbor came over looking for an escaped pig. We thought our prowler would have had to have been awfully short to pass unseen under our window . . .

To my brother,

Ruleville

Last night, I was a long time before sleeping, although I was extremely tired. Every shadow, every noise—the bark of a dog, the sound of a car—in my fear and exhaustion was turned into a terrorist's approach. And I believed that I heard the back door open and a Klansman walk in, until he was close by the bed. Almost paralysed by the fear, silent, I finally shone my flashlight on the spot where I thought he was standing . . . I tried consciously to overcome this fear. To relax, I began to breathe deep, think the words of a song, pull the sheet up close to my neck . . . still the tension. Then I rethought why I was here, rethought what could be gained in view of what could be lost. All this was in rather personal terms, and then in larger scope of the whole Project. I remembered Bob Moses saying he had felt justified in asking hundreds of students to go to Mississippi because he was not asking anyone to do something that he would not do . . . I became aware of the uselessness of fear that immobilizes an individual. Then I began to relax.

"We are not afraid. Oh Lord, deep in my heart, I do believe, We Shall Overcome Someday" and then I think I began to truly understand what the words meant. Anyone who comes down here and is not afraid I think must be crazy as well as

140

dangerous to this project where security is quite important. But the type of fear that they mean when they, when we, sing "we are not afraid" is the type that immobilizes. . . . The songs help to dissipate the fear. Some of the words in the songs do not hold real meaning on their own, others become rather monotonous—but when they are sung in unison, or sung silently by oneself, they take on new meaning beyond words or rhythm . . . There is almost a religious quality about some of these songs, having little to do with the usual concept of a god. It has to do with the miracle that youth has organized to fight hatred and ignorance. It has to do with the holiness of the dignity of man. The god that makes such miracles is the god I do believe in when we sing "God is on our side." I know I am on that god's side. And I do hope he is on ours.

Jon, please be considerate to Mom and Dad. The fear I just expressed, I am sure they feel much more intensely without the relief of being here to know exactly how things are. Please don't go defending me or attacking them if they are critical of the Project. . . .

They said over the phone "Did you know how much it takes to make a child?" and I thought of how much it took to make a Herbert Lee (or many others whose names I do not know) . . . I thought of how much it took to be a Negro in Mississippi twelve months a year for a lifetime. How can such a thing as a life be weighed? . . .

With constant love,
Heather

6 / Mr. Charlie and Miss Anne

Aside from the hate stares and the traffic tickets, the conversations which weren't conversations and the beatings, the volunteers had little contact with whites as they walked from Negro homes to Negro farms or churches or Freedom School. Many of them felt that it must be possible to do more, that somewhere in Mississippi minds could be opened.

Canton

We had thought that perhaps our one chance for making contact was through the churches. Members of our group (all white) have tried to make contact with both the white Methodist and Presbyterian Churches in Canton. The first time some of them went to the Methodist Church they had a chance to talk to a few people who really seemed to be interested in finding out what the project was all about. . . .

. . . The next Sunday they were met at the door and told by the preacher, "You are not welcome here." The third Sunday, they were again turned away at the door and beaten up on the way home. Local Negro preachers said, "Yes, that was a white man's church. It was not God's church". . . .

. . . Then a new man joined our project, Bill Monnie, who is a Methodist and is planning to study for the ministry. He wanted to make one last attempt to get into the Methodist Church. When he and several others got to the church in his car, and stepped out, a number of men rushed down off the church steps and shoved them back into the car energetically enough so that one of the car windows got broken. Two women from our group, who had gone in another car, went into the church and signed the guest book. A few minutes later an usher called them out and asked if they were connected with the COFO project. When they replied that they were, they were told they were not welcome. When they returned to the car, they found the tires slashed. . . .

143

. . . Our contacts with the Presbyterian Church have been more encouraging. Three of our group have been going there regularly. . . .

In Clarksdale on July 5 two white volunteers went to the First Christian Church (Disciple of Christ) and were refused admittance. A six-page statement was read to them in front of the church by a member of the church's board of directors while a police car circled the area.

Clarksdale, July 6th

Yesterday afternoon, Dave B. called the pastor of the First Christian Church (Dave is a disciple and plans to become a minister) and asked him for an explanation of what happened. The pastor met with us, and we had a very friendly, understanding, and mutually informative conversation. He said that he had not known anything about the incident until after church, nor had he known any such statement had been prepared. He appeared to be one of the few white moderates who is seriously concerned with the social situation, and he has been trying for five years to negotiate with some of his parishioners. . . .

Another Sunday, another church . . .

Clarksdale, July 14th

Four of us (white) went to the Episcopal Church last Sunday, and I have never felt so much outside the Episcopalian club! I tried to look nice and smile a little at everyone, so that the returning stares were discomforting. I think two people did say good morning to us. Half a block away from the church a man came up and without introductions asked us, "You won't bring any niggers next week, will you?"

If they couldn't get very far with church-goers and ministers, perhaps the "intellectuals"? Hattiesburg had its University of Southern Mississippi, a number of Jewish residents, and for sixteen years a rabbi who was known to be progressive.

Aug. 1

. . . I talked to a psychology prof at Mississippi Southern. This man is Jewish from New York, but southern orientation: schooled in Atlanta and Florida, wife from Atlanta, here since 1958. He too seemed very sympathetic, but not very willing to say anything; in fact I don't think he made any positive remarks, but he didn't make any negative remarks and smiled in the right places. I invited him to the Freedom Schools; he didn't say yes, but he did say maybe (I don't expect him). . . .

. . . Bob Beech got some Southern Mississippi prof to have an interracial group to his house, and what a comedy, with not turning on the porch lights when we came in so no one would see, and the general nervousness that none of his friends would unluckily drop by, etc. And everybody admired his courage for having us at all, which only shows what things are like . . .

Dear Mom and Dad,   July 25

Mississippi liberals are almost without exception scared stiff. Deviation from the proud old rebel flag and Our Southern Way of Life is obvious to all, and a threat or two—perhaps a few bullets fired at a house or a cross burning—is likely to leave two alternatives: silence or pulling up stakes. Boycotts are illegal in Mississippi as is handing out boycott literature, but of course this applies only to the Negroes. The Forrest County Citizens Council had no difficulty getting out a sheet calling for the boycott of several stores in Hattiesburg which had desegregated their lunch counters rather than close them down as did other merchants (after the Civil Rights Act passed) . . .
I was also told that the students did not seem to get excited about much of anything; that they were for the most part apathetic. One student told about trying to get a liberal club of some sort started last fall . . . It was about ready to go into action at the time of Kennedy's assassination but after that it died. The campus was stirred up; in some cases they cheered and gave parties celebrating the murder of the President. . . .

                                                    Bill

Dear Friends: Aug. 5

Another volunteer from the project and I sat and talked for about four hours with a dozen students; asking and answering questions. They were great kids, and most would be considered liberal in Mississippi terms—in other words, they recognize that there might be a problem, but it must be solved by the people here and the method of solution would be separate and equal. They were open and honest and we did communicate in some ways, but I could not seem to impress upon them the very basic fact of the humanity of the Negro people; their need for dignity and escape from the "great white father" relationship. As I came away from this mental beating, I cried, for it all seemed so hopeless. . . .

> In freedom and love,
> Beth

To the north of Hattiesburg, at Oxford, volunteers made a special effort to establish contact with people at the University of Mississippi.

REPORT ON A VISIT TO THE UNIVERSITY OF MISSISSIPPI

On Thursday, July 22nd, I went with George McClain, the minister assigned to our project, to the University of Mississippi—in Oxford. We went first to meet the Methodist Chaplain on the campus, whom George had met on a previous visit. He had offered to take George around the campus.

We talked with the Episcopal Chaplain, who has been active in the Movement. His great concern is for the whites of Mississippi. He emphasized that, for many people, standing up and stating their position would simply mean being forced to leave the state.

The Chaplain's feeling is that people who do believe in integration are too valuable in their communities working underground with other whites to lose if they make a principled stand and are forced to leave the state. The reason why his job is not in jeopardy, as are the jobs of ministers from congregational churches, is that he is responsible only to the Bishop of Mississippi and not to a board of local people. . . .

After eating lunch in the school cafeteria we went to visit Professor Russell Barrett of the Political Science Department. He had been James Meredith's advisor . . . He stated that he felt that there was a real lack of communication between the COFO workers and the white community. We discussed with him some of the things we were doing in Holly Springs. We then talked about getting more Negro students into Ole Miss. He said that they would all need court orders and that if we could get together some who would be interested in going to Ole Miss they could use the same lawyer and come in under the same order. He said that the Dean of Women was especially anxious to get some girls. . . .

We then went to the home of a Professor where we met a

146

student, Phil Patterson, and his wife . . . Phil Patterson had been identified as a "nigger-lover" and was eventually forced out of first one and then another dormitory by the students. The Saturday before, an attempt at a "K" had been slashed in the front seat of his car and a threatening note left. . . . The Professor's wife suggested that we come back another day and speak in some of the classes as a way of communicating to some of the students the purpose of our project. She said that she would contact some of the professors. . . .

At the Journalism Building we talked with the editors of the campus newspaper "The Mississippian." We met the girl who is editor of the paper during the regular school year, Kathryn Webb, and one of the summer co-editors, plus a few more students who were around at the time. We talked for about half an hour about why we had come to Mississippi when there were problems in so many other places, etc. Kathryn Webb was one of the most vocal in the group and one of the most open-minded. She admitted honestly that she was prejudiced and that she resented Mississippi being put in the spotlight for the summer. But she was interested in talking with us and hearing what we had to say. The others lost interest before she did and we ended just talking with her.

To sum up, we learned that there were professors on the campus actively concerned about what was happening in Mississippi. One family keeps a harassment map in their living room. The students we talked with were friendly to us although dialogue could be carried on only so far before minds began to close.

A week later, the volunteers went back—this time without their minister.

July 30

Yesterday, July 29, two of us (both white) went to speak in two Sociology classes . . . We spoke about our project in Holly Springs and then answered questions. While some questions were relevant, many were of the nature of: a "Would you marry a Negro?" "Is your oganization Communist?" and "Why are Negroes so immoral?" Both Alvin and I felt that it was fairly successful. We were able to answer most of the questions in sociological terms. The second class which we attended was an advanced class in Urban Sociology. Their questions were for the most part more sophisticated. Both classes treated us respectfully and were very attentive to what we had to say . . .

A few girls came up and invited us to eat lunch in the cafeteria with them. I was told later by a professor that this move was fairly courageous on their part, as students who had eaten with two people involved with the Movement a month before had been under pressure from their fellow students. . . . We spoke with about seven students, though none stayed with us more than 15 minutes and none offered to renew contact. There were catcalls of "queer" and "communist"; a boy who came up and said, "I heard you were on campus and I just came up to say, "I won't shake hands with you sons of bitches." Eventually we found ourselves sitting alone in a crowded cafeteria. . . . Our conversations at lunch depressed me but I could not really put my finger on why until after we had left.

When our car came to take us back to Holly Springs, two police cars followed our car to the outskirts of Oxford. They waited until we were at the edge of town. Then they stopped us—three cars, four policemen. They asked for all our identifications . . . Before he let us go, the policeman gave us a lecture about why we should notify the police when we come to Oxford, so that they could protect us from any harassment.

Even as he was uttering these words, three burly characters were walking up and down in front of us. If we had not been stopped, we would never have been seen by these guys. When we left, a green truck pulled out *right* behind us and began to follow us. We recognized the three who had marched up and down before us as we were talking to the police. Our driver picked up speed and so did they. Soon we were driving at 90 and 100 miles per hour, with them right behind us. We finally lost them when a police car passed us coming from the opposite direction and probably stopped them. . . .

Later, I realized what had been bothering me about those people at lunch. It was that they were patting themselves on the back for recognizing and admitting that conditions in Mississippi were bad. . . .

I find it hard to care about people who say they are concerned but will not take small risks to help prevent the deaths of many other people . . . I am beginning to understand why people who work in the Movement come to not really care too much about the kind thoughts of some "liberal" southern and, for that matter, northern whites.

I try to fight the bitterness . . .

But the Summer Project did assign twenty-five volunteers to work exclusively on finding white allies. Eighteen of them, including a good number of white Southerners, went to Biloxi—a "moderate" town on the Gulf Coast. Some of the group worked on making contacts with "poor whites," the rest with middle-class residents.

In midsummer, one volunteer evaluated the job they had done thus far.

Greetings from the sovereign state of Mississippi,   July 30

It looks like the pilot phase of our White Community Project is pretty much over. We had a war council over the weekend to hash out what we had learned thus far. First of all, the group of 18 of us dropped into the community of Biloxi was too big. Eighteen people, in one place, in a community which already expects all manner of chicanery from the "invaders," and watches every move so closely that little could be done. A more subtle and selective approach needs to be taken, working with smaller groups. Second, the groups should have a more specific focus. Groups attempting to be involved in the power structure and business and religious community have to maintain a different image to be effective from a group in the poor white community. We have worked against one another in this area. Those whose interest is the poor white community enabled the rest of the white community to consider us a bunch of beatniks (which they probably would have done anyway!) and at the same time, those of us involved in the middle class were always after the others to improve their appearance for the sake of our success, causing tensions within the group.

Third, in the middle class white community, a more selective approach must be taken. With few exceptions, people in business and politics and in the churches feel they cannot speak out . . . This being the case, our approach must change from the attempt to involve them in action NOW, but to explain the nature of the coming changes. . . . This new approach would be much more quietly done. It would not consider time spent with people of commitment rigidly opposed to us as very worth while.

Soren

Fear, fear, fear: the same story over and over again. It was no white myth; the volunteers themselves saw intimidation in action.

149

. . . Yesterday, four of us went to a radio station near here to leave off a tape of Martin Luther King pushing the Freedom Democratic Party. The owner was very business-like and agreed to run it 23 times for $37.50, which he is required to do by the FCC (since it was a paid political announcement). Today, he stopped by, gave us our money back, and signed an affidavit that his home and family had been threatened. It's easy to see why the white community wants to "move slow" on integration—they have nothing to gain and they have a tremendous fear of the lawless element. The whole thing has all the flavor of a TV western where there's a bad guy with a gun who's keeping everybody in town scared—well dammit, it's about time somebody faced up to the bad guy. . . .

The whites were afraid of each other, afraid of the Negroes, afraid of the volunteers.

Canton, July 7

. . . They are scared. They are terribly afraid that the Negroes will treat them the way they have treated the Negroes if the balance of power shifts. . . .

Dear people,   Batesville

One thing which has seemed plain to me, when reading the Jackson newspapers or talking to local officials, is that the whites are just as frightened as the Negroes. They have their own set of rumors. . . .

One evening I drove past an auto accident; a white girl's face has been severely gashed. At the request of her date, I went to a nearby house for help. For a moment I had a cordial conversation with the white college student who came to the door. Then he figured out who I was and rushed back into his house to get his dog and shotgun. Naturally that ended that conversation—and left the girl stranded. Sometimes I think that a hot line is needed beween the white and black sections of Batesville. . . .

Geoff

Entwined with the fear was the obsession of sex; almost every conversation between the volunteers and local white people came around to that theme in the end. It seemed to

*run so deep that the Mississippians could not bear the sight
of physical nearness between Negro and white even when the
sexes were not mixed:* "A newspaper editor told me that he
had seen one of the white girl volunteers with her arm around
a little Negro girl, playing with her hair. This, he said, almost made him vomit. The look on his face proved it was
true."

Dear Mom and Dad,   Canton, Aug. 2

Karol and I went canvassing down route 43 last Friday. On
the way back, close to our freedom school, a big sweaty white
man who looked as if he had been drinking stopped beside us
in his black Renault. We told him our names and shook hands
with him. He identified himself as Mr. Green. First he asked
if we wanted a ride, and we said, "No thank you," and said
we were headed for the church just ahead. He turned around
and followed us so we beat it into the outdoor toilet. He sat
in the driveway and honked. When we came out, he stopped
us.

"What are you two white girls doin' usin' that nigger toilet?"
he asked.

"Using it," we replied.

"We got better places for white girls around here."

"One place is as good as another."

"But not fer white gals. How old is you?"

"Twenty-two." "Twenty-five."

"I got some kids your ages. One of 'em goes to Mississippi
State."

"That's a good place to go," I said.

"You'v heered of it?"

"Sure."

"What you doin' 'round here? Are you talkin' to niggers?"

"We've been visiting with Negroes." His eyes got big.

"You're both purty gals—some of the purtiest I've ever
seed. But you know what? I seed you the other day up at thet
nigger store talkin' to the worst nigger slum in the county.
Why, that nigger slum cain't even count to ten!" and he held
up ten fingers.

"Yes, we've been talking to Negroes at the store," I said.

"We'd be glad to come to your home and talk to your wife
and you together, but we'd rather not talk here," Karol said.

"You married?" he asked.

"No."

"No."

"You reckon you'd ever make anybody a wife?"

"We'll probably get married sometime." He shook his head and dropped the subject.

"I still can't see why purty gals like you would want to go talkin' to them nigger slums what cain't even count to ten. This place ain't fit fer white gals."

"We're here because we don't like slums, either." (I hadn't quite caught on that he called people "slums").

"But them slums is plumb mean an' . . .

"We'd still like to come to your house to talk to you one day next week, maybe," Karol said again.

"I wouldn't let the likes uv yew in mah house . . .

Love,
Kay

Columbus, July 7

. . . To give you some insight into the mind of the white southerner, dig this. I'm the communications and security officer in the project here and this entails answering the telephone whenever I'm here. Following are some of the things I've been greeted with by southern white women: "Is this the place where poor white trash and black bastard niggers live together?" "Nigger, would you mind singing for me?" One day I invited a young lady to come over and we would explain in detail our purpose for being here. She said, "and get raped?"

Dear Betty,

Carthage, July 15

. . . I was in Jackson overnight Tuesday and had my first brush with the Mississippi lawmen. No beatings or anything but they weren't what you'd call polite. . . . When I told them I was a medical student, they accused me of being down here to do abortions on all of the white girls who are pregnant by Negroes. But this seems to be an obsession all across the country. One of the girls gets a letter from her father almost daily asking her "to come back home and start associating with decent people again." . . .

Sincerely,
Clarke

Dear friends,

Ruleville, July 18

Time and again they talk about how we are just spoiling a beautiful relationship. They take great pride in their solicitude for Negroes. When I ask Negroes about whether whites are just lying or really think they are good to the colored,

Negroes always answer that they are lying. They can cite cases where the very man I was talking with had beat up a Negro. What's more, the lopsided power relationship in this system makes the Negro lie to whites in order to stay alive. This lying reenforces the whites' illusion and destroys the Negro's self-respect . . .

In the ideology of non-violence we talk about being against the system, not the man. However, this is damn hard to practice, for the man is so implicated in the system that any attack on it is a real threat to him. At the same time, I don't think you'll be able to really communicate the wrongs of the system to the man on top without attacking it. The system has numerous mechanisms for dealing with challenges from within. One must find a very direct and compelling, even coercive means of cutting through these mechanisms and reaching the man . . .

Best,
Mike

In Vicksburg, a volunteer from Harvard wrote of how his ideas about white Mississippi had changed—and not changed —during the summer.

Dear people,

At Oxford, my mental picture of Mississippi contained nothing but an unending series of swamps, bayous, and dark, lonely roads. Of course the real Mississippi is nothing like that—but there was a certain logic behind my misconception. It had, quite simply, been impossible for me to believe that the skein of uncivilized atrocities that one knew had covered this state, could have spread through an area that looked as modern and developed as the places we came from.

A white lady with whom I dined one night in Vicksburg uncovered this attitude of mine. "You Northerners all think that every Mississippian is a bare-footed redneck," she complained. She and her husband had invited another summer volunteer and myself to their large, modern ranch-style home. We were eating steak, which had been cooked over a barbeque pit, and drinking wine. "Some of us are different."

All night she had been calm and charming but now, as she talked, her eyes became teary and her voice wavered. Her feelings were not hard to understand. Our characters and backgrounds had been subjected to similar distortions here in Mississippi. My hostess was no closer to the Erskine Caldwell characters I had expected to find dominating this state than

153

I was to the immoral, unwashed Communist dupe who, rumour here once had it, would persuade all Negro cooks to poison their employers' food.

I wanted to tell her all this in a tone that would leave her believing that I, a reasonable man, had come to this state and quickly seen the error of my prejudgments. But I couldn't: this state is actually worse than anything I had anticipated. I could more easily accept atrocities that took place in the swamps and woods—in pre-civilized surroundings—than I can accept the daily harassments and threats at factories, gas stations, and hotels: places which, for me, fall into the familiar context of American life.

I was eager to establish a friendship with her. But as she talked of her Mississippi, I kept thinking of the state familiar to the young Negroes I teach at our freedom school: a world light years removed from her carefully decorated ranchhouse and her excellent steak dinner.

She had told me that not every Mississippian was a barefoot redneck, and I knew she was right. Wearing shoes and a comfortable collar, a gas station owner several blocks away had fired one of the young Negroes who attend our school, and had apparently been privy to nightly threats on the student's life. I tried to mention this incident to my hostess. "I know the man you're talking about," she said. "He's one of the lower class people around here, and they're always harsh with Negroes." But was there really so great a distance between the fellow townsmen? . . . Both husband and wife undoubtedly ate, without much discomfort, at restaurants which had refused to serve Negroes weeks after the Civil Rights Act passed. If we developed this point, the distance between our attitudes would become too great, so we went on to another subject. By Mississippi standards it had been a good conversation: each of us had learned something. Yet too much stood between us. She called herself American and so did I. . . But, in her state, whenever I pause for a moment to reflect on the history of a particular person or acre, I cannot help but feel like a depressed and confused alien, and wonder whose land I am really in.

Paul

Take this hammer, Carry it to the captain.
Take this hammer, Carry it to the captain.
Take this hammer, Carry it to the captain.
Tell him I'm gone, boys,
Tell him I'm gone.

If he asks you, Was I runnin'
If he asks you, Was I runnin'
If he asks you, Was I runnin'
Tell him I was flyin', boys,
Tell him I was flyin'.

If he asks you, Was I laughin'
If he asks you, Was I laughin'
If he asks you, Was I laughin'
Tell him I was cryin', boys,
Tell him I was cryin'.

Captain called me, Nappy-headed nigger.
Captain called me, Nappy-headed nigger.
Captain called me, Nappy-headed nigger.
Ain't my name, boys,
Ain't my name.

7 / The Greenwood Story

How to convey the magic of place names unknown to the rest of America; how to explain that the map of Mississippi could become in a single summer more rich in associations, even nostalgia, than the whole geography of childhood and school—more fabulous than the cities of Europe which one might have known in another kind of summer? The young volunteers said Neshoba, McComb, Tallahatchie in a way that other generations say Barcelona, Iwo Jima, Stalingrad. Not because the Project was like a war, although it sometimes seemed that way, but because both sets of words transmit echoes of pain and courage, and images of a particular sky or earth color or human being. The words became possessions:

Batesville, July 30

Last night we gathered together from all quarters and cor-

155

ners of the county for a four-hour staff meeting. We talked about things in general, but chauvinism kept creeping in. Somehow the Crenshaw people always got the talk around to Crenshaw; the Sardis people, to Sardis; the Crowder person, to Crowder, the Como person, to Como. . . .

The names could even sound like the places they stood for: Natchez, off-limits to white volunteers, exotically evil; Pascagoula, with its slippery Uncle Toms; Yazoo City, lawless like the Wild West. Indian names, Anglo-Saxon names, a town named Midnight and a river named Big Black. The irony of names, which produced a sign in COFO offices everywhere:

> *There is a street in Itta Bena called Freedom*
> *There is a town in Mississippi called Liberty*
> *There is a department in Washington called Justice*

Each name and the place that went with it had its uniqueness, its history, and none more than the Delta town of Greenwood. At first glance it might seem typical . . .

Greenwood

"He jes' grew up on the wrong side of the tracks." The proverbial phrase is loaded with meaning for the Negro child here. The railroad tracks divide the Negro community from the white. The houses in the Negro neighborhood are perched precariously on several stacks of bricks. They are old and often unpainted, with cardboard instead of glass at many of the windows. Most often the property of whites, the houses received little attention from the owners. They are never vacant: there is no other housing for Negroes.

Yard space is at a premium—60 sq. ft. in front is almost a luxury with little more in back and none on either side. Some people fill the space with every variety of flower—the temptation to stop and smell the freshness is overwhelming. More frequently yards are bare or non-existent. A sign hanging on a porch advertises "Cockroaches for Sale" (for fish bait). Who would have to *buy* cockroaches?

In the poorer section, the yards and even the porches are gone. No series of "Good mornings" greets the white civil rights worker here, only closed doors and the frightened looks of undernourished children sitting on the steps. Many of them seem not even to have the energy to brush away the flies. Untreated cuts and vicious-looking scars already identify them as inmates of the ghetto.

West MacLaurin Street. Skid Row of the Negro district. The

five block section is broken only by one of the grade schools. The street is lined with taverns and joints. Brave talk about what "Ah's goin' a do next time Ah meet Mr. Charlie (the white man)." For all the defiant speeches and camaraderie, this area is most resistant to active participation in the movement. Fear and disillusionment brought them here and it will keep them here until tangible signs of hope appear. . . .

The statistics were familiar too: Greenwood is about half Negro, half white. It is the seat of Leflore County, whose entire Negro population (30,500) far outnumbers the white. Some 258 Negroes were registered to vote in that county as of 1963.

But Greenwood had a history of exceptional violence. Ten years earlier, the body of 14 year-old Emmett Till had been found in the Tallahatchie River which runs by the town; he had been killed just north of there in a place called Money. Greenwood was now the home of Byron de la Beckwith, twice tried for the murder of NAACP leader Medgar Evers and twice freed by a hung jury.

In June of 1962, Sam Block of SNCC had come to town. He was joined by Willie Peacock and the two went out together to talk to the people about voting. Somehow they weren't killed. But once Sam Block had to live for a week in a car parked in a junkyard because nobody dared take him in.

That fall, so many Negroes went to register that the county Board of Supervisors stopped distributing the surplus food which 22,000 people depended on. By mid-winter their situation was desperate. Friends of SNCC across the country sent shipments of food and supplies. People kept on going down to the courthouse.

In February, 1963, white men fired thirteen bullets into a car carrying James Travis and Robert Moses of SNCC, and Randolph Blackwell of the Voters Education Project, a new coordinating agency. VEP asked all voter registration workers in Mississippi to move into Greenwood immediately. In March their office was destroyed by fire. The white world didn't give an inch, but black Mississippi began to move.

This was the Greenwood to which a large group of volunteers came in 1964. A 20-year-old white Harvard student from New York tells the story of the summer in a series of letters.

Dear Family: Greenwood, June 22

Things are very quiet as of now—so quiet that the old-timers are worried. We were out this morning passing out a notice for a mass meeting tonight. All of us were followed by the police, but none were even questioned or stopped. A guy who went out to get some cartons for packing the books that are downstairs where the national office of SNCC is going to be was followed all over town, but not stopped. The theory here is that the cops are trying to convince the reporters who are still thick here that nothing is going to happen, and then lower the boom as soon as they leave for more troubled waters. . . .

By the way there is a large Chinese community here, of all things. [They are descendants of laborers brought in to build and work the railroads which connected inland Mississippi with the River when it was a major artery of commerce and travel.] They all run food stores, and about half of the stores are Chinese-run. The kids speak with a real Southern accent, but also speak Chinese to themselves . . .

The meeting tonight was really something. Over two hundred people were there and they were very hip. We all introduced ourselves. Stokely [SNCC project director for the Second Congressional District, Stokely Carmichael] gave a good speech, very sound politics. He didn't give them any of this better-street-lights crap, but talked the question of power. Power is not abstract if you know how Eastland controls the appointment of every single judge in the whole damn county . . .

July 2

Canvassing is dirty work. It is very tiring, and frankly boring after the first hour or so. (Three hours is about all most people, including myself, can stand). It is almost impossible to overcome the fears . . . And the courthouse people make sure that you have to wait a long time, and make sure that there are no chairs around. They only let three take the test at one time, in an office large enough for ten . . .

We have mass meetings two or three times a week. The trouble is that one gets the feeling that it is the same people all the time. There is a wonderful preacher around here who yells and haw-haws during the speeches. When he speaks himself he comes up with things like, "If you can't go ten blocks to the courthouse, how are you going to go nine million miles up to heaven?" and "If they don't believe in integration, how come they's so many half-white Negroes around?—somebody's been integrating for a long time."

We are planning a Freedom Day for July 16, hopefully over

158

the whole area, but at least for Greenwood . . . This consists of large numbers of people going down to register. It will mean trouble of some sort, but we have to use it to stir the community into united action. Taking a few down a day is not going to break Martha Lamb [the registrar].

July 3

Had a great time canvassing today, in spite of sour report about the boredom of canvassing in my last letter . . . Finally I have met a guy who works at the only large factory around here—Baldwin piano. Segregation works in funny ways here. Some Negro men, no Negro women. Each operation is done completely by one race or another, and the only contact is when parts are being passed from one department to another. The restrooms and smoking rooms are segregated . . .

Where else but in Miss. can you have a dry state and a tax on liquor? The cops come into a place, pick up their $100 a month apiece and a fifth of whiskey (used to be a pint) and walk out. The guys who run the cafes display their tax stickers prominently. They are called 'privilege taxes,' or something . . .

July 9

The NAACP flying wedge of integrators is not well liked around here—and I am not just talking about the white folks . . . the places they integrate are not places that the ordinary non-middle class Negro is likely to visit. Also, they must be blind not to see that places which are open to them will be closed to the ordinary Negro. No violence when the group is there with its press entourage—but just wait until tomorrow afternoon when they are hundreds of miles away. These guys also give people the idea that they have their freedom now, and can run all over the place integrating everything. Some kid tried it last night at the white movies and got beaten up by six guys. The police came and rescued him, (by taking him to the station), but did nothing to the guys who were still standing around. The same thing happened to the kid's brother, last week.

Keep your eyes open for news on July 16th—that's Freedom Day in Greenwood. One wonderful story about what happened last Freedom Day. Some whites brought a monkey down with a little sign around its neck saying: "I want to vote too." They took him into the registrar's office, but soon came out gleefully proclaiming the fact that he was refused because he couldn't read either. Then they took him across the street to

159

where the whites were because he was insulted by being on the same side of the street with the niggers. But the final laugh was on our side. Some old lady couldn't see too well, and had never seen a monkey before anyway. Nobody could convince her that it wasn't a 65 year old white woman!

We had a meeting of all Delta area people. It was really wonderful, seeing the people who seemed like old friends, even though I had only known them for a few days at Oxford. Now I understand why snick [SNCC] people hug each other when they meet. We are so glad to see each other alive and well!

July 11

It seems as if things are about to break now. The NAACP leader's tires were slashed right in front of his home last night. The night before, his windshield had been stoned for the second time. Three of the stores that carried posters announcing Freedom Day had their windows smashed. More people have been going to the white movie. Last night a group of about 5 saw most of the picture, and then it stopped right in the middle, and the manager asked them to leave and come back Sunday night. He gave them a full refund, and receipts. They left the theatre in the face of a small mob that didn't do anything except call a few names. The local NAACP guy was with them, which is very good . . .

The white swimming pool has been full of water but temporarily closed for the last week. Just yesterday, however, the city voted to give the pool to the Kiwanis Club for its members. It's gonna have a lot of white members, methinks . . .

July 13

Two snicks just got married a few minutes ago—guess we have to call it a Freedom Wedding.

The brief service was held in a little chapel on the ground floor of the office. Flowers were scotch-taped to the wall. Strings were hung from wall to wall: sprigs of spruce alternating with Mississippi Freedom Summer leaflets hung along the way. Some of the kids had spent the afternoon using glue and sprinkle-glitter things to make a cross and a Jewish star. All, including the bride, wore jeans. The service was not the usual religious one, but a personal appeal to God to guide these two children to do what is right, and so on. When it was all over, Jim Forman stood up and yelled in that wonderful booming voice of his: "ONE MAN—ONE WOMAN—TWO VOTES!"

We are going out canvassing at 4 in the morning tomorrow

to catch the people as they load up on buses which will take them out to the fields to chop cotton. (Chopping is hoeing weeds that grow after a day or so of rain, so that chopping is seasonal within a season. Picking comes later. Typical wage from 5 A.M. to sunset is about 2 to 3 dollars. And soon picking will be almost all done by machine around here.)

Some ministers arrived to take part in Freedom Day. I drove some of them to their houses just now. Driving back alone (along the road where Jimmie Travis got his) was rather scary. You imagine all sorts of cars following you. Beckwith lives in a motel down the highway, incidentally.

On Freedom Day a large number of people were taken down to register; with them went about 100 volunteers, staff and local people carrying "One Man—One Vote" and similar signs. They were testing the antipicketing law recently passed by the Mississippi legislature.

July 17th

Here is the Freedom Day special issue. . . .

Wednesday nite Stokely spoke at a very large mass meeting. He had been stopped by a well-known highway patrol goon some miles north of here, and told the folks about his interview. The cop asked him how come some niggers always laugh and smile so much, hoping to make Stokely mad. How come niggers sit on the porch, how come they drink so much and cut each other up. Stokely said "that's right—niggers drink too much—but they learned that from the white man. Niggers are lazy, and they learned that from the white man,—haven't you seen white folks sitting up on their porches?" With Stokely talking about niggers all the time, the cop couldn't get him by using the word. And Stokely said, "Now we're learning from the white man about how to vote, baby, so they'd better watch out."

In the morning, I helped coordinate the transportation to the courthouse, and went around the neighborhood trying to get people to go down to register. Went down with one car, arrived just in time to see the first group of about 30 pickets going off to jail. They had been piled into a big bus with bars across the windows. They were banging on the windows and screaming FREEDOM at the top of their lungs. Later in the morning, I got word that a cattle prod had been used, and that a 7-months pregnant woman had been dragged down the sidewalk with a billy stick under her nose.

161

Down at the courthouse, in the afternoon, the third wave of pickets was about to be launched. People waiting to register were lined up all the way down the steps. Martha Lamb was still only letting 3 people in at a time. They did allow us to bring a water cooler down for the people outside.

We tried to take a blind guy up, to test what they would do in his case. (Before, they had just refused to give him the test on the grounds that he couldn't read or write!) As I walked up the steps of the courthouse with him, one of the county sheriffs called over and asked me why I was bringing up a stupid old nigger who couldn't read or write or even walk up the steps alone. "What's the matter, don't blind people vote around here?" I asked. "Don't get smart with me, boy—I'll hand you over to my bouncer here and we're gonna whup your ass down these steps."

Towards the end of the afternoon it started to rain, not too hard at first. We decided to see what would happen if we went up on the porch of the courthouse to get out of the rain. We were thrown off, of course, back into the rain—which was getting worse. The whole gang of cops and sheriffs, up on the steps, really got a kick out of seeing people try to huddle under the few umbrellas that we had.

That night we had the largest mass meeting ever, back at the Elks Hall again. Jim Forman was the main speaker . . . I remember him talking about how it wasn't the poor white man who was doing so much against us. The guys who shot Jimmy Travis are well-known, and as Jim says, anyone who has fifteen huge tanks of Standard Oil gas is not poor. People reported having been fired that very day. And all the people there agreed that they would not work for those families. The guy who dragged the woman off in the morning has a store in the Negro neighborhood, but that won't last long now, I can assure you. Jim said that soon we have to form a community welfare fund to support people who lose their jobs for freedom.

After the meeting we had a long staff meeting that lasted until 2 A.M. We first thought that we must picket, to keep up morale, and because the people would expect it. Some feared violence, because the Negroes were certainly mad about what happened, and would fight back. Jim Bevel [of the SCLC], the wonderful reverend who wears a skull cap, was there . . . He didn't think violence was a problem. The people will believe you, he said, we used to take a bushel basket around to the gathering place for a large march and explain to the people that if a cop was cut, the whole thing was finished. They would then fill the basket with the knives the people

162

had brought. Bevel says you shouldn't keep on going to jail unless you have so many people ready to go that the whole country will take note, and you get immediate action. (We had orders from Jackson that no more staff should be arrested.) Halfway measures just run your bail up a few thousand dollars . . .

The lawyers came up with the idea that was finally adopted. We would take picket signs into the voter registration line and stand there with them. People waiting to register would carry signs saying: "I WANT TO VOTE," snicks would carry signs saying: "REGISTER TO VOTE," and so on. The people who showed up for picketing the next day agreed to this. The police drove their bus up that afternoon but didn't arrest anyone at all. They really couldn't call it a picket line, and we were definitely covered by the Bills of '60 and '64.

July 22

Much water has passed under the old dam since I last wrote. Been too busy, since we who were out of jail had to do all the work. I ended up more tired than my bed-mate, who spent the week-end in the jug. I slept at the office most of the time—on the floor—and he at least had a hard bed. Some cat came in from Jackson and they assigned him to the other half of my bed. He ended up with the whole thing, as I was at the office all night.

You probably know the story of how the city tried, convicted and sentenced all of the kids. [Over 100 had been arrested.] All got 30 days and $100 fine. We finally got them out, just before they were about to be sent onto the roads to work . . .

I went to the county farm to pick up some of the people who had been kept out there (all Negro). Aside from a one-minute visit to Stokely by one of the lawyers on the first afternoon, the whole bunch of about 50 were kept entirely cut off from all relatives, lawyers, doctors, or anyone. When I drove up, they were all yelling FREEDOM NOW and really kicking up a storm. I yelled back that we had come to get them out, and they started singing and cheering . . . As they came out, 6 at a time, they embraced us, and asked when we wanted them to go back to jail . . . 'We had a ball in there,' was the general consensus. The jailors had really had a hard time with these kids, (some of the "kids" were over 60 years old, by the way,)—they had stopped up the drains and flooded one floor. They had started 3 fires, and had torn boards off the walls and thrown them out the windows. . . .

De la Beckwith is now on the auxiliary police force, by the way. He rides a cop car with a gun and a club.

What I have been feeling for over a week now was just confirmed by a long memo from Jackson. I don't think we should spend any more time taking people down to the courthouse to get spiritually beaten down. Now we should put all our efforts into Freedom Democratic Party work. At the same time, more Mrs. Hamers and Mrs. Grays [Mrs. Victoria Gray of Hattiesburg] will be emerging as local leaders—people really capable of running the Movement and making the decisions.

Too bad I didn't go to jail and lose some weight. They had a hunger strike going for five full days.

July 26-27

A real hum-dinger of an evening. More about Jake and Silas McGhee, the two brothers who have been integrating the movie theatre. You know that the FBI made the first arrest under the Civil Rights Act in connection with the beating of Silas.

Well, they went down again tonight. After the film was over, they called and asked if we could come pick them up. Nothing doing as yet, but they didn't like to try it alone. By the time we sent an all-Negro car down there, a mob of over 100 people had gathered, and the situation was really bad. We were on the phone all the time with one of the brothers. He described the movements of the crowd, and told us that the theatre manager was demanding that they get out, since the theatre was about to close for the night. The police were there, but refused to give them any protection. He couldn't see too well whether our car had pulled up yet. Then, with 3 of us listening on different extensions, he told us that he was going to shoot his way out. It was really tense for a few minutes, as we pleaded with him. He promised to hold out until our car arrived.

Bob Zellner* and Phil M. and I jumped into another car to see if we could find out anything. We rode with windows up and door locked tight. We got to the theatre and found it deserted. Whatever had happened—had already happened. Bob leaned out of the window and asked in his deep Southern accent where were the goddamn niggers at. Nobody knew. . . .

*Bob Zellner was one of SNCC's few white Southern field secretaries.

164

We found out that they had been picked up by our car after finally getting a police escort from the theatre. As they got in the car, the police stepped back, and as if on signal, the mob rushed the car, and a coke bottle was thrown through a window—the glass from the window and the bottle cutting both brothers over the eye. They went straight to the Leflore County Hospital and were treated promptly.

Another car went down to the hospital to see if everybody was all right. That car was shot at on the way, but finally managed to get safely to the hospital.

The situation was at this time fairly bad. Cars full of whites were riding up and down in front of the hospital. Five guns were seen, .22's and .38 pistols. Later, the mother of the brothers came with their older brother, Clarence, an army man with 12 years of army experience behind him (Korean War paratrooper) in full uniform. All were holed up at the hospital.

We were very afraid the hospital would demand that they leave the place [since the two younger brothers had been discharged after treatment]. We gave our people instructions not to leave unless they got a full escort and guarantees of safety. The local police refused outright, and the Highway Patrol said it would look in on the case.

We were on the phones like mad, talking to FBI, congressmen, trying to get the Pentagon to rescue the soldier in uniform, and so on. On the phone from the hospital, the soldier told us that if we didn't get him out in 30 minutes, he was taking his family out any way he could.

By this time, the FBI had finally decided to do something. Not on their own, of course, but after many, many phone calls, and many protestations on their part that they did not protect people. Two agents came over here to see the broken car window, and to see if they could get any fingerprints from the bits of coke bottle. At least 6 agents later showed up at the hospital, very hostile but taking statements like mad.

Meanwhile, we were getting a steady stream of information from the hospital. It seems that one of the kids was beaten on his way from the theatre to the car. With a policeman standing right beside him. The cops told them that they got themselves into it, and they had to get themselves out. This while in the middle of a mob, and while one of the kids was being beaten right and left.

The Hiway Patrol and the sheriff both sent people down to the hospital and Chief Larry also went down. The soldier had been convinced to stick it out, and not try to get out the bad way. The sheriff finally agreed to escort them, but said that they would have to come over to the other side of the hospital and come out that way. To get to the other side, you have to cross the driveway where the white cars were moving around. No dice. Our people said they wouldn't move until they had a car in front and one in back and were escorted to their cars out *their* door. Finally they got an escort—and are home safe. They were headed off by a white car on the way back, but the police went over and cleared them out—the first positive action by the police during the whole incident. . . .

July 30

Two nights ago we had some real trouble over an integration attempt. Whites rode through the Negro section of town firing shots into stores, and so forth. Some Negro kids threw bottles through white car windows, and it is just lucky that enough whites were scared off before they started using the guns they all had with them. We decided that the time had come for us to organize the kids into a militant but hopefully non-violent group that would do things during the daytime—when the danger of shootings is greatly reduced. If the night riders come at night in retribution, people will shoot back in defense of their homes, Robert Williams style.

Last night we had a great meeting of local, "violent" kids, here at the office. The McGhee brothers were there, but they were not the war-hawks. I think the McGhees were somewhat sobered—but God knows not scared—by their experiences. Silas had it right: when coming out of the movie theatre, just taking the coke bottle by the neck and not shooting back saved his life. When he was pulled into the car with the white men who had lead pipes, he lived by fighting hard enough to get away.

Zellner made a key speech: "I have lived in Alabama all my childhood days, and moved around a lot because my daddy was a preacher. I had to fight every day the first couple of months, when we moved into a new town. Had to take on all the kids my size and bigger. If some joker comes up to me outside here, he may beat me up, but brother he's going to know he's been in a fight. When I'm on a picket line or in a demonstration, it's a different matter. The Man is just waiting for you to hit him so that he can put you away. You pull a knife and he'll shoot you so dead so fast, and nobody in the county will say he was wrong to do it. You go on a man's property, and he shoots you down, and no jury will touch him. I've been in 15 jails in 5 southern states, and I've

166

been beaten so that you wouldn't recognize me, so many times. . . . One time there were 500 people waiting to beat me up, and I was hanging onto a railing. 18 people were trying to pull me off, and I was non-violent as Hell holding on to that railing. All 18 of um couldn't pull me off, and I'm alive here today."

Our law student, who is about 10 times as good and hard working as most lawyers, explained the legal situation: what your rights should be, and what they are. Not everyone, by any means, was convinced. But the back of the war-hawk group was broken . . . We decided to put on a concerted effort to get Slim Henderson out of business. Slim is the cop who dragged the 7-months pregnant woman down the sidewalk. He owns a grocery store in the middle of a Negro neighborhood. We decided to go around the neighborhood with pictures of Henderson dragging the pregnant woman away. We also gave the kids Freedom Democratic Party information to hand out at the same time. After we had worked the neighborhood, we organized the kids to march around shouting: *Slim Henderson's Store Must Go!* This was very good for them, releasing some of the tension . . .

We just received another shipment from FASC. FASC is a little-known national organization: Friends and Admirers of Stokely Carmichael. We keep on getting these wild Care packages with all sorts of soap and toothpaste and candy, and those towelettes, and baby powder, and prickly heat powder and shampoo and insect repellent and shoe polish and more soap and so on. There is great merriment amongst the people who happen to be in the office when they arrive. Stokely sits in the middle of the pile and hands the stuff around and makes little comments:

"Young man, tell FASC what you want and FASC will see to it—FASC is generous and fair."

"Oh, my people saw me on TV and got a look at my shoes, and here is shoe polish: 'Yours from FASC.'"

We have a good time here when we are not getting beat up or shot at or threatened . . .

August 2

So much has been happening that my arrest seems like a small bit of information that I should pass on.

Three different cars tried to run me down when I was in a parking lot of a large supermarket registering people. A whole bunch of the not so non-violent youth started taunting a white man in one of those cars. He got out of the car and

167

started threatening them with a knife. At this point Clarence McGhee stepped onto the scene, the big brother of the two kids who have been down to the theatre. He stands well over six feet. He understands the need for non-violence, and has helped us calm some of the kids down a couple of times. But if somebody touches him—look out! Well, with thirty screaming kids standing around, daring the white man on, Clarence just stood there with a little smile on his lips, his head cocked slightly to one side, and waited for the guy. He didn't shout or taunt or anything, he just stood there and stated the facts: "You've got the knife, come and get me." The yellow peckerwood turned away, of course. The sight of Clarence standing there certainly was the prettiest sight I have seen so far in the state.

Well, then we all walked down the street, the kids still going strong, and me trying to calm them down somewhat. A cop came along and five helmeted police jumped out and told us to stop and started warning us that they would arrest the whole bunch of us if we gave them any more trouble. Just at that point a white man ran out from a store, and fingered me: "He's the one, he's the agitator, he's been causing trouble all day." They put me under arrest, frisked me, and started strong-arming me toward the car on the other side of the street. I tried to ask what the charge was, but they were shouting back at the man, asking him if he would testify, and telling what time the hearing would be. Half way across the street one of the cops hit me hard in the right rib. I thought it was a fist, but people on the street said that it was a club. I slumped down in the street, and the cop who had my arm twisted behind my back dragged me along the rest of the way and threw me sideways into the car. As we went down to the station, one of the cops turned around in his seat and suddenly reached over and pulled a fistfull of hair out of my arm. Later he yanked my snick pin off and jabbed me in the leg with it. Real kid stuff—absolutely senseless.

Two FBI men came around to the jail later and asked if I had been brutally beaten. The first bit of humor so far. I told them no, not brutally . . . Finally Chief Larry came into the cell, and said I could go.

Great trick we could have pulled on the FBI, but forgot to do. Our office was shot into [just after I got out of jail]. The FBI came and got up on a ladder to check the bulletmarks. He was sort of nervous up there, and the people down below kept on making comments about cars on the street and so on. The ladder apparently began to shake visibly, and the FBI asked whether people were watching the street all right. Dottie says she should have said at this point: "Sorry, we are not in the protection business, we will, however, investigate the matter to see if any Federal Law has been violated." That, brother, is a perfect analogy of how we feel all the time: up a ladder with your pants down, and FBI's running saying that they really can't do anything until we are messed up and something has been violated. . . .

Looking forward to seeing you all soon. Write more.

Yours in the struggle,

Bill

Another volunteer continues the Greenwood story.

Dear Folks,   Greenwood, August 17

. . . Last night at the mass meeting, Greenwood was fed a double-barrel blast of fame in the persons of Harry Belafonte and Sidney Poitier. It was a deeply exciting experience, and a strange and enlightening one. It was exciting when James Forman entered from the back of the packed auditorium after we had waited two hours and cried, "Freedom! Freedom!" and the two tall straight men moved in thru the people and their screams like gods, their faces holding the same dramatic intensity, by association, that they hold in the most effectively contrived photographs. And it was strange and enlightening when these two seemed fumbling and amateurish and, most of all, *awed* on stage, lacking the showman's composure and command. Belafonte gave a shamed, beseeching little talk about how his heart and his body as well as his money have been with the Movement since it has begun, and this is probably true. And then Poitier stepped forward and in an almost matter-of-fact but decided tone made this embarrassingly frank and dramatic statement: "I am 37 years old. I have been a lonely man all my life. . . . until I came to Greenwood, Mississippi. . . . I have been lonely because I have not found love, but this room is *overflowing* with it!"

There is the danger that I am being unjust and inaccurate with this description. But in general this is what happened; they moved from the grandiose, the sublime, toward the pathetic. We saw public figures become private ones, and we saw human beings informed more fully before us. But when I allow myself to recall this experience as I felt it, it is saddening and then almost embittering. I think it was sad because I don't feel the room was overflowing with love and their perception of it describes their need, most of all, and reveals

169

perhaps an expectation of a spiritual experience that they haven't found in the North. Also, as I said, it was embittering, because of the vision of the North that they brought with them, the "Canaan" where everybody can vote. You wonder: is freeing the Negroes to that end desirable? Is it freeing them at all? And the problem becomes insupportably large because you realize that the character of an entire nation must be changed. And it is also embittering not just to see they mistook the crowd as including ideal qualities of soul, but because my own vision of that perfect emotion has also been "tarnished" in that the crowd was people that I knew, and not "Southern Negroes" . . .

A special news bulletin has just come over the air reporting the shooting of Silas McGhee. He was sitting in his car in the Negro section and someone in a passing car shot him through his left temple. The report claims that he's in satisfactory condition, that he needs surgery, that he will recover . . . His older brother, the Korean war veteran, is now in the Greenwood jail on an assault charge which is supposedly trumped-up.

This is the next morning. Silas had driven a bunch of Snick people to a cafe after a staff meeting and was sitting across the street in one of the radio cars sleeping over the wheel. Witnesses say that a new white station wagon slowed down beside his car and shot thru the closed window and into Silas. People in the restaurant, hearing the shot, rushed out and opened the car door, and Silas fell out bleeding onto the street. They called for ambulances but supposedly none was available. The latest news is that either they could not or else would not perform the operation on him needed to dislodge the bullet. So he was driven to Jackson a hundred miles away. It is our feeling that Silas was refused treatment. A similar incident occured about three years ago when a civil rights worker [James Travis] was struck by bullets meant probably for Bob Moses right outside of Greenwood. The delay involved in arguing with the hospital and in taking him to Jackson nearly killed him. We are waiting to hear now whether Silas survived the operation. Whether he dies or not, the important point in terms of the civil rights movement in Greenwood is that they *meant* to kill him. . . .

The battleground between blacks and whites in this community recently has been the several stores owned and run by white men but patronized primarily by Negroes. The first of these to be boycotted was Slim Henderson's. Several arrests have been made during demonstrations near there and at least twice the police have stood guard all day with rifles, preventing cars from passing the store and in general attempting to frustrate the boycott. This man has nearly been run out of business.

A boycott had also been started on a man who tore down a civil rights sign that was posted across the street, who has supposedly been "fresh" with his girl customers, and who has cheated those customers of his who are on credit. Another woman, who has claimed that she would shoot dead anyone who tries to boycott her store, has successfully boycotted herself by threatening everybody with a shot-gun. That has been a scene out of Faulkner, this lean woman with straggly hair brandishing that huge gun, levelling it now and then at the crowd and watching them run. She has fired it several times, so far always high in the air. Now she threatens to drive the streets shooting at every civil rights worker she sees. . . .

The Student Nonviolent Coordinating Committee places a large order when it asks people to meet this kind of violence with non-violence. So far in Greenwood, they have been able to make their point—that non-violence is tactically necessary in demonstrations and wherever the ends of "the movement" are concerned. But SNCC has also, I think, encouraged self protection, and it has proven difficult to discern where self-defense and "defense of the community" are distinct from each other. To these young people, as to most, violence has usually been, in the minds of Southerners, to be courageous. The boycott, powerful economic blow or not, does not satisfy the repressed urge of these young people to strike back. Silas' shooting last night came close to touching off unspeakable things . . .

I am enclosing a statement that one of these boycotted storeowners made over the radio . . . It is very frightening to know that anything *they* do they justify on bases of principle, and to realize that much of what they do is inspired by moral fervor. Playing on their sense of guilt is a dubious, even negligible weapon, it would seem. I saw this perverted moralism translated into violent action the other day when I was chased out of the white neighborhood with stones and curses, a car finally ran me off the road and forced me to dive into a Negro's chicken-coop for safety. That little gimp-legged man with the wild blue eyes who was not a good enough shot to hit me with the rocks, who ran after me down the street with his cronies, who roared after me in his car and came up onto the dirt after me with it, who swung at me with his left hand as he went by but missed again, believed that he was striking blows for freedom, among other things—for all that is good and right. I suppose all you can do for a man like that is pray for him. Is he wicked? If he isn't, then maybe no one is and maybe that's the proper conclusion: there are no evil men in the world, only scared ones and indignant ones and hateful ones. But if there are no evil men, there *is* evil; you feel it come into yourself when you view these men. . . .

Love,
Bret

Silas McGhee lived.

We are soldiers
in the army
we have to fight
although we have to die

We have to hold up
the freedom banner
we have to hold it up
until we die

Freedom Song

8 / *Philadelphia,*
August Third

Greenwood, June 29

We have heard rumors twice to the effect that the three men were found weighted down in that river. Both stories, though the same, were later completely dropped in an hour or so. How do you like that guy Gov. Johnson saying that they might be hiding in the North or maybe in Cuba for all he knew . . .

Tchula, July 16

Yesterday while the Mississippi River was being dragged looking for the three missing civil rights workers, two bodies of Negroes were found—one cut in half and one without a head. Mississippi is the only state where you can drag a river any time and find bodies you were not expecting. Things are really much better for rabbits—there's a closed season on rabbits.

Como, August 3

About three weeks ago there was a flying rumor that they had been found in a rural jail. Tonight it was said that three graves had been found near Philadelphia. How the ghosts of those three shadow all our work! "Did you know them?" I am constantly asked. Did I need to?

173

The bodies were found on August 3 and identified the next day.

Last night Pete Seeger was giving a concert in Meridian. We sang a lot of freedom songs, and every time a verse like 'No more lynchings' was sung, or 'before I'd be a slave I'd be buried in my grave,' I had the flash of understanding that sometimes comes when you suddenly think about the meaning of a familiar song . . . I wanted to stand up and shout to them, "Think about what you are singing—people really have died to keep us all from being slaves." Most of the people there still did not know that the bodies had been found. Finally just before the singing of "We Shall Overcome," Pete Seeger made the announcement. "We must sing 'We Shall Overcome' now," said Seeger. "The three boys would not have wanted us to weep now, but to sing and understand this song." That seems to me the best way to explain the greatness of this project—that death can have this meaning. Dying is not an ever-present possibility in Meridian, the way some reports may suggest. Nor do any of us want to die. Yet in a moment like last night, we can feel that anyone who did die for the Project would wish to be remembered not by tributes or grief but by understanding and continuation of what he was doing . . .

As we left the church, we heard on the radio the end of President Johnson's speech announcing the air attacks on Vietnam . . . I could only think "This must not be the beginning of a war. There is still a freedom fight, and we are winning. We must have time to live and help Mississippi to be alive." Half an hour before, I had understood death in a new way. Now I realized that Mississippi, in spite of itself, has given real meaning to life. In Mississippi you never ask, "What is the meaning of life?" or "Is there any point to it all?" but only that we may have enough life to do all that there is to be done. . . .

At the Freedom school and at the community center, many of the kids had known Mickey and almost all knew Jimmy Chaney. Today we asked the kids to describe Mickey and Jimmy because we had never known them.

"Mickey was a big guy. He wore blue jeans all the time" . . . I asked the kids, "What did his eyes look like?" and they told me they were "friendly eyes" "nice eyes" ("nice" is a lovely word in a Mississippi accent). "Mickey was a man who was at home everywhere and with anybody," said the 17-year-old girl I stay with. The littlest kids, the 6, 7, 8 year olds, tell about how he played "Frankenstein" with them or took them for drives or talked with them about Freedom. Many of the teen-age boys were delinquents until Mickey went down to the bars and jails and showed them that one person at least would respect them if they began to fight for something important . . . And the grown-ups too, trusted him. The lady I stay with tells with pride of how Mickey and Rita came to supper at their house, and police cars circled around the house all during the meal. But Mickey could make them feel glad to take the risk.

People talk less about James Chaney here, but feel more. The kids describe a boy who played with them—whom everyone respected but who never had to join in fights to maintain this respect—a quiet boy but very sharp and very understanding when he did speak. Mostly we know James through his sisters and especially his 12-year-old brother, Ben. Today Ben was in the Freedom School. At lunchtime the kids have a jazz band (piano, washtub bass, cardboard boxes and bongos as drums) and tiny Ben was there leading it all even with his broken arm, with so much energy and rhythm that even Senator Eastland would have had to stop and listen if he'd been walking by. . . .

And Andrew Goodman: he had been in Mississippi little more than twenty-four hours.

On August 7, James Chaney's funeral and memorial service took place in Meridian.

Meridian, August 8

. . . The service was preceded by several silent marches beginning at churches throughout Meridian and converging on the First Union Baptist Church. I have been on a large number of walks, marches, vigils, pickets, etc., in my life, but I can't remember anything which was quite like this one. In the first place, it was completely silent (at least, the march I was on), even though it lasted over 50 minutes, and even though there were a fair number of children involved. . . .

Meridian, August 11

. . . In the line I was in, there were about 150 people—white and Negro—walking solemnly, quietly, and without

175

incident for about a mile and half through white and Negro neighborhoods (segregation is like a checkerboard here). The police held up traffic at the stoplights, and of all the white people watching only one girl heckled. I dislike remembering the service—the photographers with their television cameras were omnipresent, it was really bad. And cameras when people are crying . . . and bright lights. Someone said it was on television later. I suppose it was.

Dave Dennis spoke—it was as if he was realizing his anger and feeling only as he spoke. As if the deepest emotion—the bitterness, then hatred—came as he expressed it, and could not have been planned or forethought . . .

Dear Folks,   Laurel, August 11

. . . The memorial service began around 7:30 with over 120 people filling the small, wooden-pew lined church. David Dennis of CORE, the Assistant Director for the Mississippi Summer Project, spoke for COFO. He talked to the Negro people of Meridian—it was a speech to move people, to end the lethargy, to make people stand up. It went something like this:

"I am not here to memorialize James Chaney, I am not here to pay tribute—I am too sick and tired. Do YOU hear me, I am S-I-C-K and T-I-R-E-D. I have attended too many memorials, too many funerals. This has got to stop. Mack Parker, Medgar Evers, Herbert Lee, Lewis Allen, Emmett Till, four little girls in Birmingham, a 13-year old boy in Birmingham, and the list goes on and on. I have attended these funerals and memorials and I am SICK and TIRED. But the trouble is that YOU are NOT sick and tired and for that reason YOU, yes YOU, are to blame, Everyone of your damn souls. And if you are going to let this continue now then you are to blame, yes YOU. Just as much as the monsters of hate who pulled the trigger or brought down the club; just as much to blame as the sheriff and the chief of police, as the governor in Jackson who said that he 'did not have time' for Mrs. Schwerner when she went to see him, and just as much to blame as the President and Attorney General in Washington who wouldn't provide protection for Chaney, Goodman and Schwerner when we told them that protection was necessary in Neshoba County . . . Yes, I am angry, I AM. And it's high time that you got angry too, angry enough to go up to the courthouse Monday and register—everyone of you. Angry enough to take five and ten other people with you. Then and only then can these brutal killings be stopped.

176

Remember it is your sons and your daughters who have been killed all these years and you have done nothing about it, and if you don't do nothing NOW baby, I say God Damn Your Souls. . . .

Dear Blake, Mileston, August 9

. . . Dave finally broke down and couldn't finish and the Chaney family was moaning and much of the audience and I were also crying. It's such an impossible thing to describe but suddenly again, as I'd first realized when I heard the three men were missing when we were still training up at Oxford, I felt the sacrifice the Negroes have been making for so long. How the Negro people are able to accept all the abuses of the whites—all the insults and injustices which make me ashamed to be white—and then turn around and say they want to love us, is beyond me. There are Negroes who want to kill whites and many Negroes have much bitterness but still the majority seem to have the quality of being able to look for a future in which whites will love the Negroes. Our kids talk very critically of all the whites around here and still they have a dream of freedom in which both races understand and accept each other. There is such an overpowering task ahead of these kids that sometimes I can't do anything but cry for them. I hope they are up to the task, I'm not sure I would be if I were a Mississippi Negro. As a white northerner I can get involved whenever I feel like it and run home whenever I get bored or frustrated or scared. I hate the attitude and position of the Northern whites and despise myself when I think that way. Lately I've been feeling homesick and longing for pleasant old Westport and sailing and swimming and my friends. I don't quite know what to do because I can't ignore my desire to go home and yet I feel I am a much weaker person than I like to think I am because I do have these emotions. I've always tried to avoid situations which aren't so nice, like arguments and dirty houses and now maybe Mississippi. I asked my father if I could stay down here for a whole year and I was almost glad when he said "no" that we couldn't afford it because it would mean supporting me this year in addition to three more years of college. I have a desire to go home and to read a lot and go to Quaker meetings and be by myself so I can think about all this rather than being in the middle of it all the time. But I know if my emotions run like they have in the past, that I can only take that pacific sort of life for a little while and then I get the desire to be active again and get involved with knowing other

177

people. I guess this all sounds crazy and I seem to always think out my problems as I write to you. I am angry because I have a choice as to whether or not to work in the Movement and I am playing upon that choice and leaving here. I wish I could talk with you 'cause I'd like to know if you ever felt this way about anything. I mean have you ever despised yourself for your weak conviction or something. And what is making it worse is that all those damn northerners are thinking of me as a brave hero. . . .

Martha

Laurel, August 11

. . . As I was riding on the bus back to Laurel from Meridian after the service, all this kept running through my brain, along with the fact of knowing that nobody has ever been brought to justice in Mississippi for all those murders, that the Federal Government just bought some property with Beckwith for $27,000.00 (almost like Barnett's handshake after the first mistrial). No, the FBI is only an investigative body . . . the Justice Department can do nothing . . . Welcome to Mississippi, the Magnolia State . . . Help Save Your Country, IMPEACH EARL WARREN . . . Six months sentence, suspended to take care of tobacco crop . . . It isn't nice to have a stall-in . . . two more churches bombed . . . it isn't nice to picket the President . . . wouldn't have happened if they stayed in their part of the country . . . it isn't nice to block a door . . . white grand jury refused to indict . . . It isn't nice . . . kill 'em, burn 'em, kill the bastards . . . it isn't . . . Not Guilty . . .

I gave Kay a laugh the other night. She came into the kitchen about midnight and I was sitting there eating cold lima beans and humming "We Shall Overcome". . . .

9 / The Nitty Gritty

Dear Ruth and Carl,   Holly Springs, August 9

It is Sunday, and I have driven over 2,000 miles in the last three days. I am tired. I want to go very much to a movie, or to watch TV even. I want to be in Berkeley and do stupid things and don't look behind me in the rearview mirror. I want to look at a white man and not hate his guts, and know he doesn't hate me either. I want to talk about the White Sox and be admired by somebody who isn't going through worse than I am. I want to get out of the 90 degree weather and go swimming . . .

Love to you,
Bob

Getting down to the nitty gritty: the facts, the realities, the how-where-when-who of carrying out a big idea. The important problems have been described by the volunteers in other chapters; the smaller ones could seem just as bad.

Dear Mom & Dad,   Holly Springs

It is a little easier working within the Freedom Schools but you still have . . . the pressure of a group of almost forty living fairly closely and the tempers and moods of your leaders and the guys in the field who sometimes find release for their tension by attacking others . . . One of the hardest things is that you almost never have a chance to take a break. Sundays can be one of our hardest workings days as everybody goes to church and some don't get back until late afternoon. . . .

Wayne's death exhausted all of us [Wayne Yancey, a Negro volunteer killed in an automobile accident]. Very few were actually close to him but his death was so useless and wore down our nerves. I think that all of us have felt in the back of our minds a little nagging thought that sooner or later someone would have a serious accident. Our project is responsible for about seven counties in northern Mississippi and we have had a number of minor accidents. The constant worry about policemen and hostile cars plus fatigue make the chances for accidents much greater. . . .

Love,

Pam

Carthage, August 9

I *cannot wait* to discuss something besides civil rights. Sometimes we make conscious efforts to discuss Plato or what's the best color for toilet paper—but it's useless. In thirty seconds we're back to C.R. . . .

Meridian, July 25

I'm a Northern white intellectual snob. I can't do anything at all about the Northern or the white part; I try (believe it or not) to subdue the snobbery; but I'm a college intellectual phoney by choice . . . And in my short range of rather sheltered experiences, I suppose I have never spent this much time in such a culturally sterile place . . . I got a letter from Dave today describing the most outrageous and absurd Mahler Cycle with which he was torturing our neighbors once again, and I must admit, the thought of listening to 7 of those symphonies, more or less one after another, has never been more appealing to me . . .

Dear All,

Carthage, July 14

Transportation is still our main problem. Farms are far apart—sometimes miles; roads are terrible, etc. One day Hank and I rode mule bareback. It was all I could do at first to hold on with my legs around his belly . . . Soon I got the hang of it and did all right—didn't hold on or anything. Then a farmer gave Hank a horse and saddle, which he has been riding for two days all over the place. Talk about saddle sore, Hank the cowboy has to even sleep on his stomach. . . .

Love,

Judy

Hattiesburg, 3:30 A.M.

Boy, love life around here is really something. My experiences wouldn't make even *Junior Catholic Messenger* . . .

Dear Gretchen,   Clarksdale, July 7

I'm sitting in a junkyard. It used to be a cotton stamping and processing plant. Some of the plant is still in operation, but most of it has collected dust, debris and rust . . . Next to the yard is a clearing and a group of Negro kids are playing soft ball—without gloves, without shoes and without bases.

I went walking to try to get away, but I can't. Wherever I go, I see kids without shoes; wherever I go, the air is heavy. The tension has subsided a great deal in Clarksdale, but there is no escape from the psychological and physical poverty . . .

In many ways this reminds me of camp. In the first weeks, kids and problems will be of special interest and they will be a constant topic of conversation. Later, people get sick of talking about the same problems and topics and start making jokes about it to get away from it. Conversations seem superfluous unless you find a person with whom you may be comfortable. There is no one I can relax with plus there is no place to relax and forget about problems that you no longer want to think about or waste words on . . .

Hope to hear from you soon.

                                                Lew

                                                Gulfport

The roads are clay and dusty. Red dust that kicks up when the breeze passes. It gets into your clothes and your hair. The red mud on the side of the road left over from yesterday's rain storm clogs your shoes and somehow leaves stains on your pants. But somehow none of this matters when you are welcomed into a person's home and talk to him about registering for the vote . . . And so clothes cease to be a real concern. "Image" ceases to be a real concern. If it ever was. In spite of the National Council of Churches' advice, we crap on the clean, antiseptic, acceptable, decent middle-class "image." It is that decency that we want to change, to "overcome." It is that decency which shuts these "niggers" in their board shacks with their middle-class television antennas rising above tarpaper roofs. So crap on your middle class, on your decency, mister Churches man. Get out of your goddamned new rented car. Get out of your pressed, proper clothes. Get out of your unoffensive, shit-eating smile and crew-cut. Come join us who are sleeping on the floor . . . Come with us and walk, not ride, the dusty streets of north Gulfport . . .

Life in a Project "office" had its own special quality.

Gulfport, June 24

The SNCC shack is across the road, a two room wooden shack, plastered with pictures of Freedom candidates and CORE and SNCC posters. One room is just beginning to be an office, with five typewriters and a mimeograph machine and newly installed windows. The other room is devoted to sleeping—with mattresses on the floor. . . .

Leland, August 10

The present office is upstairs in a place called the "Athletic Club," a place that is neither athletic, nor a club, but does sport a small "snack" bar, where beer and wine are served, and in the back of the place is a long room where card playing takes place, a juke box is ensconced, and some dancing is done among the small clientele. Upstairs is our office-bedroom combination . . . we are not plagued with any of the normal problems, such as rats, mice, and cockroaches, or even mosquitoes—the reason is very simple—we have miniscule ants that literally infest the damn place, eat all refuse that happens to be left around . . .

Perhaps the hardest part of being an office worker was the sense of being removed from the action, behind the front. Yet nothing could have been more important than the work of the communications people, particularly at the COFO headquarters in Jackson.

Dear parents,   Jackson, July 3-6

This office is almost beyond description. Hot—the air-conditioner is still broken [the only one in a Project office], very full of people doing very important things apparently without any order. The office is one long room partitioned by plaster board. No windows! Perspiration runs down the back of my legs at 4:00 A.M.! Plywood desks are nailed to the walls around the room. Dogs, paper, pop bottles, glasses, newspapers and people are strewn everywhere. A visitor would see no order in the madness, but it *is* there. With the difficulties of the first week and the very busy job of dealing with the press and trying to perform as security agents for the entire project, we had little time to think of organization. Things are looking better, however. I am generally impressed by the ability of the leadership though I find it necessary to exercise my own judgement. The Negro SNCC workers know how to be 'cool'; some of the whites think they do, and don't. But that is a small matter.

I am very happy tonight, though I have had no sleep in 2 days, hardly, and only one meal today. We in communications have the responsibility of running the telephone system and handling the press, knowing where everyone in the state is. We are the security system. The FBI, local police, Justice Dept, press from around the nation, are our constant 'phone companions. Since I am now chief WATS operator, I will describe to you how it works. The WATS is a "Wide Area Telephone Service." It costs about $500 a month to have a state WATS line but you can make an unlimited number of calls around the state per month. By means of the WATS line we are able to keep in close contact with the projects across the state. Almost all information that comes into the office comes over that phone. It is absolutely essential to security and transfer of all information. The WATS operator types up all vital data received in the conversations she has with the field concerning a million different things. The WATS line digest is compiled from these typed reports. There is another WATS line used for program calls which involve long discussions of detailed plans. There is also both a state and nation-wide WATS line in Greenwood, where the SNCC headquarters is located . . .

This evening I happened to be the one who answered the phone to hear "emergency" from Moss Point. One more incident you will see in the morning paper about the 'battle for civil rights in Mississippi.' The strange thing is that even here in the heart of the organization and of the state, I have a hard time believing what really goes on. . . .

Love,
Margaret

Jackson and Greenwood were headquarters for the security system, but "security" was a mystical word which haunted Project workers all across the state. Some workers considered the do's and don'ts very important; staff members often had less patience, especially with the sign-out, sign-in system, which applied equally to a hop down to the corner for a pack of cigarettes or a 20-mile trip into dangerous rural territory.

In mid-July, an important new safeguard was added. . . .

Our security precautions are as good as they could be. The house is set back about a hundred yards from the road, and there are three searchlights which are kept on all night. We also have two dogs, appropriately named Freedom and Now respectively. The most effective precaution, though, is the new 2-way radio. I've learned to use the code numbers and names. We use it whenever anyone goes any distance from the house or at night, checking in at each destination and giving estimated times of arrival, etc. One girl walked home tonight as it was getting dark—with the radio. I wasn't too happy about it, but she seemed to know what she was doing. She called once or twice, because a car was following her for a while, but it turned out all right. . . .

The two-way radios were installed in cars as well as offices, using the "Citizens' Band" which operates on 23 frequencies. Whites did some jamming, but destroyed only one installation, in Natchez; they seemed to prefer to fight back by increasing their own supply of two-way radios.

Sometimes the volunteers slipped away from all the tensions for a while—to New Orleans for friendly white faces and legal bourbon or to Hodding Carter's swimming pool in Greenville. But then the old problems might come along too . . .

Clarksdale, July 12

I went to Mound Bayou with four Negroes—it is an all-Negro community about 28 miles south of Clarksdale. We just talked, drank, ate fried chicken and danced. It was a night of relaxation except for the fact that we kept discussing the Negro problem and the Jews—since they asked me if I was Jewish. As we talked and drank, tongues got looser and out came Negro resentment towards whites—misconceptions like all whites have money—but Negroes are still better, etc. They think they're all hip—which is true—and that whites want to be hip like them—which is sometimes true.

The tension at Oxford between volunteers and staff members, whites and Negroes, did not vanish in Mississippi. The northern white volunteers were less awed now than at orientation; they had fresher energy than the veterans, less patience with a casual approach to the job, and often a strong leadership drive. Usually they were better educated and better "adjusted" than Negroes in the Movement: local people as well as staff.

. . . Several times I've had to completely re-do press statements or letters written by one of them. It's one thing to tell people who have come willingly to Freedom School that they needn't feel ashamed of weakness in these areas, but it's quite another to even acknowledge such weaknesses in one's fellow workers. Furthermore, I'm a northerner; I'm white; I'm a woman; I'm a college graduate; I've not "proven" myself yet in jail or in physical danger. Every one of these things is a strike against me as far as they are concerned. I've refused to be ashamed of what I cannot change; I either overlook or purposely and pointedly misinterpret their occasional thrusts of antagonism; I think twice or more before asserting myself or pronouncing *my* opinion on any affair in which they have more experience, and so far have had no really unpleasant moments at all . . .

"No bad moments at all" does have one exception—a run-in with a 17-year old fellow who's been with the Movement in the south since '60, has served countless jail sentences, was a participant in the bloodiest of Freedom rides and considers himself, rightfully so, a true veteran. He's quite loud and swaggering and hypersensitive to criticism or insult (imagined or real). One afternoon he was knocking away (literally) at a guitar with neither knowledge nor talent. The guitar's owner (a white boy) appeared and requested the instrument. Request ignored. Owner *took* it away. Injured feelings flamed immediately into anti-white tirade that was carried on for 15 minutes straight. I had been trying for the last hour to write a report and was getting very tired of the racket. So I foolishly asked the ranter why he didn't join the Muslims if he so badly hated the white man's guts. No rational response, just further venom directed at us. I'd given him a new target—a white woman. My temper ran away with me at a certain remark from him and I childishly commented on his super-friendly behavior toward certain other white gals. . . .

Love,
Jo

Another problem has to do with a local volunteer, an ex-drunkard who is finding something in life in the movement. He has a great need for being in the center of attention, and is usually arrogant and spiteful to all he meets. In one of our staff meetings he came in drunk and started attempting to take over the meeting. George put to us an ultimatum:

either agree with him or else he would leave the group. After he walked out, many of us felt that he would be harmful to the movement if he stayed, but the NCC minister with us, a very gifted and articulate worker, brought up the question of just what our purpose was down here and just how we had failed if we could not help George rather than lose him, if we could not have some respect for his problems. The rest of us soon fell to attacking ourselves for our attitude, and we talked about what we had done wrong and what we could do. It was a beautiful act of what we are here for—to build a society where the problems of the individual can never be forgotten, a world where understanding and love are the keys to success. . . .

Ruleville, July 27

. . . The question is how much energy and resources can we exert in helping people like this, who have personality problems, and still meet the tasks that have to be met. So far we haven't been able to give them much constructive attention. It is frustrating to know that you can't be an effective caseworker with our resources and thus must continually avoid getting really involved in people's personal problems . . . However, I find the broad attack on the system much more satisfying than the case work approach. . . .

Yet amidst all the tensions, the moods of irritation and despair, perspective remained.

Hattiesburg, July 27
(Written on an opened-out paper bag)

I got a letter from a boy in Altadena who wants to come here for the rest of the summer. It was sort of a strange letter: he wakes up in the night with just one word pounding in his heart and his head. The word is *Mississippi*. He wants more than anything to come here. I wrote asking him to question his motives, and if he thought he had reasons instead of just feelings for going to Mississippi, he should come . . . The boy wrote that he called you. Encourage him to come if you see fit; my letter may have been discouraging . . .

Go tell it on the mountain
over the hills and everywhere
go tell it on the mountain
to let my people go

10 / Democrats for Freedom

Clarksdale, July 22

. . . The heat the last two days has been so unbearable that work has been virtually impossible . . . Harassment continues at a low level but steady . . . Voter registration has been stalled for over a week—the registrar has closed the courthouse . . .

The one bright spot is the Freedom Democratic party . . .

Dear friends,   Greenwood, August

To my way of thinking, the most exciting aspect of this summer is the politics of it, especially the grass roots elements of politics down here.

The Freedom Democratic Party, which accepts the political processes of America, including party politics, is something even newer than other forms of political action such as demonstrations, sit-ins, freedom rides, etc. A freedom ride or demonstration has short-term, usually symbolic goals. When a person sits in at a hamburger joint, he is protesting discrimination in all white public accommodations. But it is time now to go after the long-range goals of political power through direct participation—through the right to vote. This must be done by the FDP, because the Negro is denied these rights in the regular Mississippi Democratic Party.

Until court orders finally demand it, the registering of Negroes on the official books of the state seems a hopeless task: 94% of the eligible Negroes in Mississippi aren't registered. Old Martha Lamb, the official registrar of Leflore County, just won't give in to the waves of black faces which confront her every day. Earlier this month, three Congressmen came by to observe voter registration practices in Miss. A young Negro girl, age 24, had tried to register nine times in the past three years. Each time she failed. When we asked her to try again,

187

she broke down in tears, saying she just couldn't take any more degradation. However, Bill Ryan, one of the Congressmen, demanded to see her back tests. (We were never allowed to see them ourselves.) He felt strongly that her answers were better than some of the whites who had passed. So Ryan convinced her to try again. (We learned later that she *did* pass, with Congressman Ryan breathing down Martha Lamb's neck. She was the only Negro to be registered in Leflore County all summer.)

Because official registration is hopeless for the moment, we are concentrating our efforts on FDP registration. But this is tough too. The Negro community in the South, particularly Mississippi, has had absolutely no political education. And whenever he has tried to take the bold step into politics, he has been beaten back into submission and kept in ignorance. The closest thing to politics around here is church elections when they elect Deacons . . . As for the expression of interests and needs through the political process, the Negroes are totally inexperienced. If nothing else is accomplished this summer, at least a good education in politics and political expression will have been achieved by the Negroes, paving the way for more effective action in the future. . . .

I still feel, and always will, that political power is the most powerful instrument of peaceful, legitimate change. And as the Negro gets the vote, he gets representation. With representation, the powers of the state must begin to look more to his interests, and as the whites adjust to this power change, then progress is made on all fronts. They don't have to love each other, but they do have to accept the realities of change.

The FDP meets the standards of a regular party. Its meetings are open, its meetings are documented. Legal proof, showing not only voter intimidation by the whites of the regular party, but also the qualifications of the FDP meetings and elected delegates, is being gathered and sent to the Credentials Committee of the Democratic Convention which starts at Atlantic City on August 24. But besides meeting basic requirements and being open, we have a larger claim to acceptance by the National Democratic Party. We support the national party and its platform and candidates. The regular Democratic Party does not. Senator Eastland of Mississippi has voted against most of the major bills proposed by this administration. This time, the regular Mississippi Democratic Party will probably not support Johnson . . . When the FDP presents its legal and political credentials to the National Credentials Committee, these credentials should be accepted. If not, the

188

Negro in the South is left with few other avenues of expression.

The FDP is a product of imaginative and responsible thinking. Hopefully, the American people are still imaginative enough to accept this move . . .

Best regards,
Phil

Although both regular voter registration and organization of the Freedom Democratic Party had been carried on simultaneously from the start, by late July the emphasis of the Summer Project had almost totally shifted from regular registration to getting people "Freedom registered." A simplified form was used, modeled on that of a northern state, and the purpose was to show how many people would register if they could in Mississippi. Their numbers would support the convention challenge at Atlantic City.

The underlying idea of the FDP was as real as grits, but it didn't always seem that way to a volunteer standing on somebody's porch trying to explain the national Democratic Party and Mississippi Democratic Party and Mississippi Freedom Democratic Party and how they were related thus and so. On the other hand, Freedom registration had the advantage of being secret—unless the police arrested a worker and seized his forms, which happened once in a while. But still. . . .

Greenville, August 19

One of the difficulties is that most Negroes in Mississippi are instinctively apprehensive of the word "registration." They connect it with going to the courthouse and answering a lengthy trickily worded form. Also, some ask if they have to pay any money, associating it with the poll tax which is still required in state elections in Mississippi (the 24th amendment to the constitution of the U.S. applies only to federal elections).

Dear Mom, Dad and Vickie,   Rural Madison County, July 28

Yesterday we canvassed . . . One lady couldn't work because she had cut her leg badly with the hoe while chopping cotton, and her leg was full of stitches. She lived in a two-room unpainted shack (kindly provided by the management). You climbed on the porch by stepping on a bucket—there were huge holes in the porch for the unwary. The woman was sitting dejectedly on the bed as she couldn't walk very well. She was surrounded by shy children, some of them naked . . . We tried to explain what Freedom Registration meant—it seemed like a rather abstract approach to her problems. . . .

Another time, we were walking behind the church where we have our Freedom School and saw the gleam of a rooftop between the trees and heard children's voices. I went back and asked the Negro girl who had come with us if it would be all right to visit the house and she said "Yes." So Karol, Minnie Pearl and I undid the latch and walked down the lane. Tall pines lined the road with blackeyed susans and great elm trees in between. The house, if you could call it that, was made of unpainted boards . . . three planks served as porch steps. Two little girls on the porch disappeared into the house as we reached the gate. A woman in a ragged dress looked out of the door and told us to come on in . . . Several children who looked about the same age came out to see us, their little stomachs sticking out with the bloated look of starvation and their eyes dazed and listless. Inside a baby cried. I asked the mother how old the baby was and she said two months and added that her oldest was seven. She had six children. I started explaining about the Freedom Democratic Party and she listened, saying "yes mam" to everything I said. . . .

The construction of the place was very shabby and would have been unbearably cold in the wintertime. The house belongs to a white man whom the couple works for. They work in the cotton fields from 5 A.M. to 5 P.M. and when I asked what they do with the kids while they are in the fields, the lady said "We have to take them with us." The seven-year old, she said, takes care of the baby. . . . She signed a Freedom Democratic Party registration form, but I'm not sure she understood it. I found out her age when I filled out the form for her—she is only 22 . . .

Love,
Kay

Dear Folks,   Columbus, August 1

The state quota for Freedom registration is 100,000, but with only about three weeks to go there are scarcely 50,000 forms in our Jackson (main) office. . . . In Columbus, where for some reason the people are more apathetic and afraid (for their jobs, not physically, I think), a good day's work was twelve forms. In West Point, where I am now, I have gotten 29. Most of the time you harp on education and jobs, and, if it's an old person, on relief ($50 per month). The

190

hope for a better future ("I'm too old, I'm going to die soon") or a better future for children ("But I don't *have* any kids" or "They're all up North.") . . . I stop at one house and find someone who not only nods, but says "That's true" or interrupts with complaints of his own and who signs and maybe takes one for his wife, and a few for his mother and father. The more prosperous houses probably mean good luck, with one major exception. Any teacher in the schools is absolutely unsignable . . .

Love,
Joel

The first test of the FDP undertaking came with the precinct meetings, which would elect delegates to county meetings; then the counties would choose people to send to caucuses in each of the five Congressional districts; and finally the FDP state convention would be held—in other words, a parallel structure to existing party organization.

Vicksburg

Fear reigned at first—but soon people were excited about the prospects of the party and neighbors were talking to neighbors about the "New Thing." Block Parties and mass meetings were being held many times a week in various parts of town. Spirit grew. Hundreds of people risked their lives and jobs to come. Representatives were elected after the election of a permanent chairman and secretary. Resolutions were introduced, minutes were kept . . . The precinct meeting was one of the most exciting events of my life . . .

Dear family, Greenwood, July 22

Last night we had the FDP precinct meeting for Leflore County. We got some of the community leaders together and had a workshop with them on how to run the meetings. The meetings were run by the local people, with snicks as 'parliamentarians.' We gave advice and assistance when needed.

We had to go through a lot of red tape getting people seated in the right areas in the hall, and making sure they were freedom-registered. This was very much worth it, though, as it gave the people some feeling of being in a real organization. The meeting hall was done up like a convention hall. There were placards for the different precincts, and banners proclaiming LBJ FOR PRESIDENT, and ONE MAN—ONE VOTE, and so on. The place was jammed, and bits and pieces of the audience were lit by powerful TV lights, giving a wonderful appearance of activity as you went in. The delegates all wore different colored tags to identify them as precinct members.

Martin Luther King spoke before the meetings. He said lots of fancy things, many of which—I think—were over people's heads. Fantastic use of metaphor. "The cancer on the body politic," etc. And he had some specific things to say . . . "Mississippi doesn't worry about states rights when they receive more than twice as much aid from the Feds as they send up in taxes. It's only when it gets down to the Negro that the Federal Government is overstepping." . . .

Freedom now,
Bill

Greenwood

What a meeting it was—a totally unorganized group of people had come together for the first of many steps in organizing a local political party. And it was truly democratic. Hundreds of people came from each precinct, compared to the five or ten Mississippi whites who show up for their precinct meetings . . .

Dear folks,   Columbus

The precinct meeting was the first political experience for those who attended, and we were sure that the job of explaining to them nominations, delegations, resolutions, would be impossibly complicated. It was tremendously interesting to watch and indicative, I think, of the innate political nature of all men. Within ten minutes they were completely at ease and had elected a chairman, secretary, and ten delegates to the district convention in Tippah. The delegates were teachers, housewives, packinghouse workers, a toy factory worker, in short, a genuine cross-section of the community . . .

Love,
Joel

Greenwood, August

Of even more significance than the precinct meetings was the County meeting. Here all the delegates from Leflore County met, and a real convention was held with candidates vying for election—with serious discussions of issues and of problems facing the community, the county. You should have seen me after the meeting. I was so excited that I kept running around outside. I was overwhelmed by the history of the meeting! . . .

Moss Point, July

. . . The County convention was held here last Saturday. It was just amazing seeing these people, many, or rather most, of whom have never had any experience at all in politics running the meeting, electing the people and passing resolutions for a state platform. These people, housewives, unskilled workers, many, but not all, uneducated, are fantastic. People who have never spoken publicly before get up and make the greatest speeches . . .

Vicksburg, August 3

After those great precinct meetings which I told you about on the phone, the county convention was a disappointment. The Old Guard—the Warren County Improvement League— the comfortable middle-aged "We Don't Want Any Trouble" Uncle Toms—monopolized the meeting and the votes. Most of the Great New Blood which pulsed through the precinct meeting was slyly siphoned out. It was a sad night for all of us. We had forgotten that machinery is quickly formed even in something as new as the FDP and our defenses were down . . .

Carthage, August 3

I went to Meridian Sunday for the District Caucus—4th District . . . there is an aware, sophisticated group creating the Party, so the extreme lack of sophistication on the part of the delegates was, for now, unimportant. It would be very easy for a small group of people to control the party, but there is no such group and the leaders really want this to be a learning event for the people . . . One man from Neshoba was elected a delegate to Atlantic City—there were three at the Caucus from Neshoba, and they got a great round of applause. It was a vision of things to come, the whole day. . . .

Meanwhile, the regular Mississippi Democrats held their state convention in Jackson on July 28. Not a single Negro delegate attended. To support the FDP challenge of discrimination, Negroes had attempted to participate in the regular Democratic precinct meetings around the state on June 16, and a week later in the county meetings. The results were as one would expect: exclusion by intimidation or trickery.

Goldwater support was so rampant at the state convention that it adjourned until after the National convention, thus avoiding commitment to the Democratic candidates and platform. This came as no surprise: in 1948, the Mississippi Democrats had bolted the national party convention. In August of 1960, they had rejected the Kennedy-Johnson ticket and platform, and successfully campaigned for unpledged electors who then voted against that ticket. And in 1963 they had issued campaign literature for Governor Paul Johnson which stated: "Our . . . party is entirely independent . . . of any national party . . . long ago separated itself from the National Democratic Party . . . both the National Democratic Party and the National Republican Party are the dedicated enemies of the people of Mississippi . . ."

About a week later, the FDP held a very different kind of state convention.

August 6, 1964

From the floor of the State Convention of the Mississippi Freedom Democratic Party:

This is the most exciting, moving, and impressive thing I have ever had the pleasure of witnessing—let alone be a part of.

Miss Ella Baker presented a very stirring keynote address. She hit very hard upon the necessity for all the delegates to work and study very hard so they can prepare themselves for the new type of fight—a political fight. She also put great stress upon the fact that these people here today have braved extreme danger and now must redouble their efforts to get all their neighbors to join them in this struggle for Freedom.

Right after Miss Baker's speech, there was a march of all the delegates around the convention hall—singing Freedom Songs, waving American flags, banners and county signs. This was probably the most soul-felt march ever to occur in a political convention, I felt, as we marched with a mixture of sadness and joy—of humility and pride—of fear and courage, singing "Go Tell It on the Mountain," "Ain't Gonna Let Nobody Turn Me Round," and "This Little Light of Mine." You would just about have to be here to really feel and see what this means to the people who are here.

Attorney Joseph Rauh, a member of the Credentials Committee of the National Democratic Convention, who is going to present the legal case for the Mississippi Freedom Democratic Party at the National Convention, then addressed the group. Mr. Rauh is also Walter Reuther's attorney and his appearance indicated the support of Mr. Reuther who is, of course, one of the powers of the Democratic Party.

Mr. Rauh presented quite an optimistic picture concerning the chances of getting the FDP seated in Atlantic City, explaining that if the Credentials Committee does not want to seat us it will only take the support of eleven members of the 108-member Credentials Committee and the support of eight states to get the matter onto the floor of the convention where we will almost certainly win the fight . . . Bob Moses didn't seem so confident. President Johnson is afraid he will lose the whole South if he seats the FDP. My own opinion is that we will not be seated, but will have won partial victory by exposing the terrible situation in Mississippi, and by forming some groundwork for progress in later years. . . .

The delegates then elected and ratified the district choices of delegates to the National Convention. There will be 44 delegates and 22 alternates going . . .

Moss Point, August 9

Thursday I was in Jackson at the state convention of the Freedom Democratic Party. Man, this is the stuff democracy is made of. All of us here are pretty emotional about the names of the counties of Mississippi. Amite and Sunflower and Tallahatchie have always meant where this one was shot, where this one was beaten, where civil rights workers feared for their lives the minute they arrived. But on Thursday Amite, and Tallahatchie, and Sunflower, and Neshoba didn't mean another man's gone. They meant people are voting from there, it meant people who work 14 hours a day from sun-up to sun-down picking cotton and live in homes with no plumbing and no paint, were casting ballots to send a delegation to Atlantic City. As the keynote speaker said, it was not a political convention, it was a demonstration that the people of Mississippi want to be let into America . . .

Love,
Rita

No Negroes had attended the regular state Democratic convention, while at the FDP state convention a white man— Rev. Edwin King—was chosen National Committeeman (Dr. Aaron Henry became Chairman). However, the total number of white FDP delegates remained small.

Dear friends,   Greenwood, August

The FDP is not for the Negro alone. It is for everybody.

195

Every person over the age of 21 has the right to join the FDP. But it is difficult to get whites to register. We can't canvas the area, because that means that we will have to go up to their door steps and on their property, where there is a good chance that we'll get shot . . .

At the moment, three whites in Greenwood are registered. What we are left with, then, is that legally we are in fact an open party, despite the small number of whites who will register with the FDP. We have attempted to publish every day, starting two weeks in advance, the date, time and place of our precinct meetings. When we wrote to the *Greenwood Commonwealth*, the local newspaper, requesting them to print our notice in their announcement column, accompanied by a very good letter to the editor, we were answered by the editor in go-to-hell terms, and our notices weren't published. All correspondence relating to FDP is being notarized and will be presented to the Credentials Committee as proof of our being open. Whites don't come to the FDP meetings, but this is their choice (not the other way around), and we have done our best to encourage them to join us . . .

Phil

There were some volunteers who tried to do more.

Dear folks,   Greenwood, July 9

It is not enough to say that we do not discriminate against whites, we must have absolute proof that will stand up in the credentials committee, which is run just like a court of law. Stating that we *would* have, if we *could* have, is a statement of INTENT, and intent does not hold much weight . . .

I have written a leaflet which I want to take into the white community. It explains the FDP, and invites people to join. Leafletting a place doesn't involve an incriminating contact on the part of the white man who is leafletted, for most of the leaflets will be left in his mailbox. The National Office is in favor of it—but the staff here is dubious of risking it. I will read the draft to a full staff meeting tonight and see what the final decision is. My plan is to take four white kids and a car into white neighborhoods in a precinct which includes parts of the Negro community. Two people to a house, four people to a street, the car following them. If we are careful, no one should get beaten up. At the end of the summer we will be able to call the leaflet exhibit x, and say that so many hundred were distributed in the white Greenwood community. Incidentally, we will never be able, nor want to be able, to tell the National Convention just how many whites we have. We do not believe in keeping separate records, as you might guess . . .

Love from the struggle,
Bill

De Soto County, July 21

Usually when we canvas, we ask where the white folks are on the road—and avoid them. This morning, there were two white families on the road and I was considering talking with them. Reports from Negro neighbors made it clear they weren't rabid, so after consultation with the group I decided to try to sign them up for the FDP.

At the first house were Mr.—— and his wife. I asked if I could come in and talk. The folks were poor white and cordial . . . I told them right off who I was . . . that I was in Mississippi because there was injustice and too many lies. I told them some of the lies about the happy Negro, about the civil rights workers, the poor white—that the poor white was stupid and violent. We both laughed at the idea that he would jump in his pick-up and look for someone to shoot if he heard of civil rights activity (heh heh). He murmured concern about the violence that actually took place. His wife wandered off to let her husband do the talking. I then talked about how the rich white played the poor white and Negro against each other. They were receptive and friendly but the man couldn't read or write and was somewhat embarrassed about being illiterate; he was still in the same economic state as the Mississippi Negro. He finally said he wouldn't sign because he wasn't too sure of what he was doing, and told me to talk to his neighbors . . .

Next door was a woman, several baby-doll type southern girls, one of them 21. There was a visitor from Arkansas who looked very unfriendly—about 30, complete with red neck. This family was even poorer than the first. By this time I was close to shaking visibly. Mrs. —— was friendly. The man from Arkansas was not unfriendly. The girls were giggly. I talked much as I had at the first house about their economic plight. Mrs. —— showed strong racist attitudes, but of ignorance not hate. I hit each one of the myths she raised with common sense and she was forced to laugh with me. She signed after I made great pledges of secrecy and security—she didn't want any of those white idiots shooting up her house. She seemed to be most convinced by my arguments about roads and the rich power structure.

The volunteer returned. At the second house . . .

Mr. —— was home; he was working on a car and talking to some friends. I went in to tell Mrs. —— of the meetings of the FDP. We were soon joined by an eighteen-year old Mississippi racist, who told me in no uncertain terms what he thought of niggers and what I was doing. His entire performance throughout the visit was fascinating; he made all sorts of threats in a vague hypothetical way; he spoke of what would happen to someone who did such and such— while continually offering me the potato chips and popcorn he was eating. After listening to this cat for a little while I went out to talk to Mr. ——. From that point on it was a constant battle to get across to the receptive Mr. —— over the little punk . . . eventually the punk turned out to be an asset: Mrs. —— and the eighteen year old niece started to take my side, at first out of friendliness. Then, as he got more ridiculous, they themselves became responsible southern moderates . . . They were even clear-headed enough to back me up on the miscegenation hangup, insisting that it wasn't the issue . . . Mrs. —— finally was won over to the party; he said he would sign because he didn't see any harm in it. As I left he told me to be sure to come back. . . .

But these were rare exceptions.
The total number of people registered in the FDP—60,000 —was not as high by the time of the national convention as Project workers had hoped. A number of volunteers made quick trips home to press for support of the FDP by their local Democratic leaders. The challenge began to look serious: by mid-August the Democratic committees of ten important states had adopted pro-FDP resolutions of varying strength. There seemed to be enough support at least to get a minority report urging recognition from the Credentials Committee— and a floor fight.

I'm looking forward to the convention. I'm not sure what our chances for success are, but we seem to have the Mississippi delegation worried. They have a court injunction against the Mississippi Freedom Democratic Party and have been serving injunctions on all the local leaders to keep them from participating. It seems they've found an old law which would prohibit our using the word "Democratic" . . .

But neither the injunction nor the jailing of the chairman of the FDP's Executive Committee, Lawrence Guyot, stopped them. They came: sixty-eight determined Mississippians plus many volunteers and staff people. The modest, almost shabby Gem Hotel was their headquarters; many of the staff slept on the floor of a church.

What happened then, between August 23 and 26, went beyond the greatest expectations of all those young people who had trudged the backroads with their registration forms, worrying about quotas. It justified all the dreams of developing indigenous leadership in black Mississippi. There, by the sea, across from a huge billboard with a picture of Barry Goldwater and the inscription "In your heart you know he's right" (later someone wrote in underneath, "Yes—extreme right"), a band of people from nowhere brought the machinery of a powerful national party to a halt for four days. They told their stories of oppression and terror—Mrs. Hamer, fired the day she registered, later beaten unconscious for voter registration work—while the Credentials Committee listened and the Mississippi regulars made feeble replies. The nation watched it all on television: the FDP had become the only issue at the convention.

They watched in Mississippi too.

Dear people,   Batesville, August 25

Black Batesville is perhaps the most politically conscious community in the country today . . . Every house glows with its little, blue-gray television light. Not just to see Mr. Miles or C. J. Williams or Mrs. Lloyd or Reverend Middleton on the convention floor, but to watch the entire fight. Bull Connor is hissed when he talks Birmingham-tough and the Michigan delegation is cheered when it announces that it will support the Green compromise—unless something better is offered. People who still pronounce "registration" as "restoration" use with understanding terms like "credentials committee" and "eight states needed for a floor fight. . . ."

                                              Jim

The complex story of what happened behind the scenes at Atlantic City belongs to another book. For this record, the Credentials Committee adopted a "compromise" which provided for the seating of the regulars; the recognition of Dr. Aaron Henry and Rev. King as delegates at large from the FDP and all others as honored guests; a promise that the

Democratic National Committee would obligate states to select delegates for 1968 in a non-discriminatory way and that it would establish a special committee to aid states in meeting this standard.

The Mississippians rejected the compromise, in the face of arguments voiced by such national figures as Bayard Rustin and Martin Luther King (who were present) that it should be seen as "a great victory." There was a sit-in by the FDP delegates. The volunteers, who had been busy lobbying for support and taking part in a round-the-clock vigil on the boardwalk, helped in this too.

August 30

At 7 P.M. we met . . . and arranged a system of runners to bring badges from regular delegates inside the hall to FDP delegates outside. I was appointed to receive badges inside and carry them outside to a person who passed them on to delegates waiting in small groups on street corners near the hall. I made about four or five trips in and out—it was really exciting. I felt like Mata Hari and the French Resistance and the Underground Railroad all rolled into one. I had very little trouble getting back into the hall, because I wore a press badge which was honored. Just to disguise myself further I wore a red, white, and blue striped vest of the kind worn by the Young Citizens for Johnson who were roaming around . . .

All in all, I think we came off rather well at the Convention. We got lots of sympathy and we didn't compromise ourselves by accepting a phony compromise . . .

Why was the compromise "phony"? The FDP had several reasons for rejecting it. The two seats were considered token recognition—and the Negro people of Mississippi had seen too much tokenism in their time. They had come there as true representatives, not as "delegates at large." The compromise still recognized the regulars, despite the mass of evidence to prove they had no business there. The promises for 1968 offered no genuine relief because they referred only to Negroes already registered; even if a few Negroes could attend party meetings four years later, the people were no more likely than before to have a voice in decision making. The compromise contained no precedent for eventual recognition or patronage. To the FDP, it was a one-shot affair—their anguish, their demands, their cause, were not.

This morning, Sunday morn, I was just in the middle of doing some washing when in marched Mrs. Hamer, sweat beading her face, dressed in old flat shoes and a short cotton dress gathered from the bodice so that it just flowed round her huge form, her hair plaited in half a dozen tiny braids standing out from her head. She embraced me the warm southern way, and launched into a high-powered, oft-times bellowing account of the Convention in Atlantic City.

She told how she had finished her speech by asking the question that was being asked all over the country: "Is this America?" She spoke of the effect of the exhibit of the car and the photographs of the three young men, of the way in which the vigil on the boardwalk grew from 18 people to 3,000 and of how Negroes and whites alike came to say how much it meant to them. She insisted, and I'm sure she's right, that next year the FDP will be the regular party. She said how disillusioned she was to find hypocrisy all over America. She felt Johnson had really showed his hand against the FDP by preventing a floor fight. She declared that King, Roy Wilkins, Bayard Rustin, James Farmer, and Aaron Henry had been willing to sell out the FDP by their willingness to accept the compromise. However, when I urged the wisdom of not splitting ranks, she said that at the end all of these people had congratulated them on their sit-in . . . She insisted that the FDP would have been prepared to split the votes with the regular Democrats, but that two votes at large was no deal.

On Friday night here at the mass meeting I realized that for southern Negroes, Mississippi Negroes especially, to see that crowd sitting down meant something that would have been completely lost if a compromise had been accepted that simply hushed everything up. One woman at the mass meeting said, "I looked at that Convention from the time it started. All the time til now I never seen no nigger in a convention, but they was there! Lots of them! Big ones and little ones, they was there!"

This may be the last time
This may be the last time
This may be the last time
May be the last time, I don't know. . . .

11 / The Road Back

Dear Ruth and Carl,   Holly Springs, August 9

Our director, a Negro, has been assigned to Yazoo City, and only the two of us are left. My mind is getting all on edge over leaving. I am abandoning the best people I ever met. It is a genuine hangup to face this responsibility. How much can I cater to my own desires, how long can I wait, how much disengagement—even to become a lawyer—is justified? Depending on what should be irrelevant considerations, my answer changes momentarily.

We had a slew of people depending on us in DeSoto County and we got pulled out to go to Tippah to start the FDP there. The same dependence developed, and we had to leave there. I let down new friends, people who risked their lives and families to let us have a floor to sleep on, and suddenly we disappear. We might be dead, and there is no communication to tell them we are sorry. But the work had to be done in two places and we had to leave. We returned to both places and people were hurt. They were worried. We had let them down. It was the right thing to do, but it hurt. What shall I do? You just keep wondering, and then an important decision comes and you make it. Then you start wondering all over again.

Show this letter to Mom and Dad, and tell them I love them more than ever in all my life (I'm learning).

Love to you
Bob

Dear Family,   Batesville, Aug. 13

I must tell you that I am reconsidering my decision to return to school this fall. As I told you before, the question of continuing my work in Mississippi has been on my mind for quite a while . . . My involvement here is quite deep. I find that I have some talent for this sort of work. . . . I can organize, explain, and I have found that I'm able to keep my head when I need to. When the project director went to Jackson last week, I was left in charge.

There is the question of my not being Negro. Ideally, us white folks could go home this fall, and Negroes could run things. But there are not enough who can. I can see a job that needs to be done and I can do it.

Occasionally one gets very lonely down here. I go downtown and see the Illinois Central train which could take me all the way to Chicago. The idea of riding from here to Chicago is sort of strange. I could just get on a train, ride, and be back in a free country . . . I really don't know what to do. I'm going to meetings in Jackson next week for those interested in staying, but then I'm coming home for a while to decide.

Love,
Gene

As early as mid-July, many volunteers were already debating whether to stay on at the end of the summer or go home—which usually meant going back to school. They dreaded an outburst of retaliation against the local people after their departure in the fall. And in fact by mid-August violence had already accelerated. On August 8, the Jackson Clarion-Ledger issued an open invitation with its banner headline: "COFO WORKERS TO ABANDON STATE ON AUGUST 24." The story was false, but the weekend which followed its appearance seemed an evil dream come true—bombings, shootings, cross burnings across the state.

The volunteers wrote home pleading with family and neighbors . . .

People of Winchester: Mound Bayou, Aug. 16

. . . Violence in Mississippi this summer had been avoided because of terrific pressure brought upon the political and economic power structure of Mississippi. This has been done through the President, through Congressmen from various Northern states, through the words of Northern industrial powers. This pressure must be continued, must be made even stronger . . .

You should realize, I think, that the President did not send more FBI agents into Mississippi, send the Justice Department into Mississippi, exert pressure on Governor Johnson, just because of a great humanitarian surge in his breast. If that had been the case, the federal government would have been in Mississippi three years ago, seventy years ago . . . The President acted this summer because he knew that there were a lot of parents, relatives and friends who had power and influence . . . He realized also that he could not afford to be forced to send troops into Mississippi. He will react to your letters . . .

Larry

Some of them decided to go home or on vacation briefly and then back—to Mississippi. Others returned to school as planned, thinking it the longer but better road back to this Mississippi or another. And some made no bones about being glad to get out of the state and back home.

Dear Friends,   En route back to Meridian, September

Many people, including those who supported my going to Mississippi as part of the Summer Project, and those who believe that the Summer Project has been an important thing, have expressed shock and disapproval at my decision to go back to Mississippi, and have attempted to dissuade me from returning. I have been amazed at this response.

There is a certainty, when you are working in Mississippi, that it is important for you to be alive and to be alive doing just what you are doing. And whatever small bit we did for Mississippi this summer, Mississippi did ten times as much for us. Working there has given me clarity about what I want to be learning in college that three years in Widener Library could not give. Now that I have taught, I know what I want to learn about teaching. Now that I have helped people understand what it means to be a citizen in a democracy, I know things that I still have to understand. Now that I have worked with people to change the society in which they live, I know what I want to learn about societies and how other people have changed theirs.

I guess the thing that pulls me back most are the people who made us a part of their community. People I knew in Mississippi could honestly and unselfconsciously express affection in a way that few people I know in the North are able to do. They did not have to be "cool" or "one up" or "careful" . . . In Mississippi I have felt more love, more sympathy and warmth, more community than I have known in my life. And especially the children pull me back. . . .

I should tell you that it is not as easy to go back to Mississippi as it may sound from this letter. I am frightened by the probability of much greater violence . . . I will be working a lot more on my own, and it will probably be much lonelier. . . .

Gail

Greenville

For awhile it seemed that nothing I could do would be more important than staying directly active in the Movement. What I have decided is, I must learn much much more about political theory, philosophy, etc. I am not sure I can stay in art. What I would like to do is finish at BU in art—then go on to some kind of profession. Maybe medicine if that's not too too preposterous. Think what a doctor who was dedicated to the movement could do. At least I want to be in some position—a valuable one—where I would come in contact with many people all the time.

Dear Mom and Dad— Ruleville, August 3

I know you are very concerned that I finish college, and you fear I may not if I stay out a year. I am very concerned that I finish college too, but I want to take a year off to stay in Mississippi . . . I want to take it now so the year I have left in college will be more meaningful, so I won't be in college just to be graduated . . .

I found that Swarthmore is a dried-up hell unless one knows what one wants to do with what one gets from school. I'll go back next year even if I don't get a better idea from a year here, because I know the diploma means security and I'm no good to these people if I'm starving too . . . A year at Swarthmore now will make me hate education and get me a diploma. A year of directed learning will make me more able to pursue whatever field I choose in the long run. I'd be miserable and waste a great deal of your money at Swarthmore. I must stay now. I will go back in September 1965.

Much love,
Gretchen

In Canton, there was a 21-year-old volunteer from Galesburg, Illinois and Knox College. Johns Hopkins had granted her an impressive fellowship for graduate work in history, to begin in the fall. When she first came to Mississippi . . .

Dear John and Cleo,   Canton, July 13

. . . Leaving Galesburg was terribly hard; I fell wrenched irreparably away from all that was helping me grow and be strong and seek faith. Probably it was good to plunge immediately into this; no chance for drowning in self-pity. . . . Maybe when this is over and the urge to introspection can be honored again, I won't hurt so much as I did when the bus pulled away with me one Thursday night not too long ago. . . .

                                                    Jo

Dear John and Cleo,   August 24

Some of them are beginning to realize, now that we're talking about the end of school and our departures, that we're not saviours and we're not staying forever and we're not leaving any miracles behind. We've awakened great expectations and now will vanish leaving folks with only a deepened sense of their destitute state and a deepened longing . . . When we talk now with our pupils about college and scholarships they respond as if we are telling fairy stories. . . .

                                                    Jo

Dear John and Cleo,   August 24

I now realize (after a couple of sleepless nights and a couple of solitary walks—despite security) and various attempts to ignore or rationalize away my strongest impulses —that nothing short of staying on here, becoming permanent staff with $10 per month which others are and have been living on—nothing short of this will satisfy me. . . .

I made my decision the night before I was scheduled to leave. I sat down to answer your letter and found myself writing that of course the end of the Summer Project is not an end of progress in Mississippi. But it's no thanks to the departing volunteers that it's not an end, it's thanks only to those who are staying on. At that point I threw away that letter and wrote to Barker and the dean of the graduate school at Johns Hopkins . . .

Maybe the immediacy of the sufferings and dangers here *is* overwhelming me and blurring out the essential "larger view," but I can simply no longer justify the pursuit of a Ph. D. When the folks in Flora have to struggle to comprehend the most elementary of materials on history and society and man's larger life, I feel ashamed to be greedily going after "higher learning." And when I feel the despair of youngsters who can't even get through high school because cotton planting prevents them, I almost feel ashamed of my college diploma. And when I reflect on the terrors and deprivations in daily lives here, I cannot return to the relative comforts and security of student life.

My love for the people, the hurt I felt when 50, 60, 70 year old men and women would plead with me to keep on with the school. . . . I knew that it would be living a kind of lie to leave here now, lamenting about how terrible leaving was and yet leaving anyway. . . .

I've been trying quite seriously to dredge up all possible motives and pass judgment on them. I think often of a little story told by Bayard Rustin—he was participating in a vigil for peace and was fasting, when he saw a huge woman walk by and suddenly realized that one reason he was fasting was his desire to lose weight. I suspect that some of my motives in this situation may be no more worthy . . .

Love,
Jo

Dear John & Cleo,   September

The man who was to have been my advisor at Hopkins has written that neither is he overwhelmingly surprised at my present action nor will he be overwhelmingly surprised if I begin looking toward Academe again in a year or two. There are some moments even now when I'm almost sure he's right, but other moments when I'm equally sure that I'll never feel like settling down into the isolation and discipline of student life again. I suspect, tho', that some sort of synthesis is possible eventually and that maybe I can become a sort of rabble-rousing scholar. . . .

Love,
Jo

Those who did not stay had several kinds of feelings.

Dear Mother and Father: Gulfport, August 12

I have learned more about politics here from running my own precinct meetings than I could have from any Government professor . . . For the first time in my life, I am seeing what it is like to be poor, oppressed, and hated. And what I see here does not apply only to Gulfport or to Mississippi or even to the South. . . . The people we're killing in Viet Nam are the same people whom we've been killing for years in Mississippi. True, we didn't tie the knot in Mississippi and we didn't pull the trigger in Viet Nam—that is, we personally—

208

but we've been standing behind the knot-tiers and the trigger-pullers too long.

This summer is only the briefest beginning of this experience, both for myself and for the Negroes of Mississippi.

Your daughter,
Ellen

Hattiesburg, August 18

Somehow, as I prepare to leave tomorrow, knowing that I will be easily integrated again into society, I wonder if I will have the perseverance to keep on trying hard to change society. Maybe I'll just fall back into line . . .

Columbus

You write that big parties are being arranged for the returning volunteers. This is a mistake. Everyone should be staying down here . . . to give the movement strength. . . . People might have decent reasons for not staying, but the people who really need support or deserve "glory" (if anyone deserves glory) are those who are staying . . . A hell of a lot of the volunteers who never planned to stay, are staying. The rest (me included) know they ought to be. Reasons for not staying are easy to amass, but everyone, including the rationalizer himself, suspects these reasons. We can't feel as though things are solid enough to keep going without us. It's impossible to justify quitting now, because this is really only the start. Nothing is conquered; no project is completed; some summer volunteers have to leave, and that's nothing to celebrate.

The first days back in the North were strange.

Late night, August 25-26, Memphis, Tenn

We drove up to Memphis this noon, and I sat in the Greyhound bus terminal for a few hours. At a barber shop I suddenly realized that the barber was the first strange white man to come so close to me in months. He worked swiftly—how different it was from the leisurely hour hair cut Mr. Whiting gave me in Como. I felt uncomfortable with white folks; I was seeking out the Negroes to talk with in the waiting room . . .

August 31

My first day back, I found a group from Downtown CORE

209

raising funds for Mississippi on the corner of 8th Street. I stopped to talk with one of the fellows and after a few minutes I began to feel odd. . . . Suddenly I realized what it was: he was a Negro, and we were on a corner crowded with white people. If we'd been in the white section of Hattiesburg, there would have been real danger.

A few days later, I was headed for the "downtown" train—in Hattiesburg that meant the white business district.

I've felt depressed since I've returned. I don't know how much is personal, and how much it is reaction to that place and the people I've left behind, and a heightened awareness of so much that is wrong up here. . . .

Chicago

As we got into our car a lean Negro squatted down by the window next to me and warned us not to leave. This was his territory, he boasted. "We may be bums, but if you want some wild excitement we can find it for you." When we told him that we were just looking for some friends, he changed his pitch. "See those guys down there," he pointed to a gang at the end of the block, "there's Eskimo, and that's Shorty and Johnny. I'm Blackboy. I'm the boss." In a moment of innocence I stuck out my hand. Blackboy ignored it.

"As long as you're with us," he continued, "you're safe anytime you come down here. We'll even watch your car for you. Ask anybody for Blackboy. But mostly just look for this"—he held his wrist up to the window, baring a silver studded leather strap. . . . "You won't see another one like it around here. Just give us seventy cents for a drink." Blackboy was in his middle thirties. He wore a blue windbreaker and blue jeans. I gave him a quarter and a half dollar, and we were allowed to leave.

Blackboy rules the four blocks south of Ohio Street on Clark Avenue in Chicago. In Mississippi we might at least have communicated. One friend of mine remarked that he was upset every time he passed a Negro—they don't come to embrace you for what you've done, and up here you can't even wave without being counted queer. But Blackboy is real too. . . .

Harrison, New York, August 30

I find that whenever I meet someone around home who hears I've been to Mississippi, he says "Oh, what was it like?" People want a nice handy three-word phrase to be able to repeat to neighbors . . . They ask me a question, then start talking before I can answer. And I grope to find words to explain what it was like—but can't.

Back in the Southland, the Summer Project had become the Mississippi Freedom Project. Some 200 volunteers—"old ones" from the summer plus new people—carried on the programs. The FDP was already preparing for a Freedom Vote in November and the congressional challenge of 1965. The bombings and jailings continued; everything seemed different, yet the same. Philadelphia, the town of death, had changed in one notable way: workers were living at a new project base there.

Dear Mom and Dad,   Philadelphia, October 4

As I write this letter I am on the roof of our headquarters observing a sunset I cannot even begin to describe. The hills of red dirt, the pine woods, the mountains and shacks silhouetted against the blood-red sun and clouds, all this and the rest of it takes my breath away. Now and at all such times I find myself possessed by a deep melancholy, a heart-rending feeling for the black and white toilers of this state; both victims of a system that they neither created nor flourish under.

There have been incidents of violence and intimidation but they hardly seem worth noting at a time like this. I only know that I must carry on this struggle that other people have died in, and that some day that system will be changed. . . .

                                        Love,
                                        Tommy

The Volunteers*

Joel Aber
Jeff Acorn
Jim Adams
Russell Allan
Kathie Amatniek
Lawrence Archibald
Ellen Argimbau

Doug Baer
Doug Baty
Joel Bernard
Jacob Blum
Bret Breneman
Virginia Brown
John Bundy

Jacques Calma
Wilfred Carney
Virginia Chute
Barry Clemson
David Cleverdon
Michael Clurman
Geoffrey Cowan
Paul Cowan
Dave Crittendon

Margaret Dobbie
Bryan Dunlap

Mary Edelen
Joseph Ellin
Nancy Ellin
Eugene Erickson

Gail Falk
Bob Feinglass
Glenn Fetty
Tom Foner
William H. Forsyth

Hardy Frye
Aviva Futorian

Lester Galt
Robert Garafolo
Clark Gardner
David Gelfand
Mary Sue Gellatly
Marylou Gillard
Allan Gould
Bonnie Guy

Jan Louise Handke
Robert Hargreaves
Albert Hausfather
Kathleen Henderson
Gregory C. Hewlett
Philip Hocker
William Hodes
Martha Honey

Lucien Kabat
James Kates
Joe Keesecker
Parrish Kelly
Richard Kelly
Paul Kendall
Michael Kenney
Howard Kirschenbaum
Adam Kline
Ruth Koenig
Rita Koplowitz

Ellen Lake
Ira Landess
Roger Lauen
Robert Lavelle
Brian Leekley
Sara Leiber

* This is not a complete list of the volunteers to the Mississippi Summer Project of 1964, but only includes those who submitted letters for this book.

Betty Levy
Mark Levy
Joseph Liesner
Michael Lipsky
David Llorens

Robert Mandel
Tom Manoff
Robert Masters
Marianne McKay
Ronald Meservey
Judy Michelowski
Steven Miller
E. Beth Moore
Philip Moore
Grace Morton
Barbara Mutnick

Karol Nelson
William Ninde

James Ohls
Joann Ooiman
David Owen

Jerry Parker
Pam Parker
Susan Patterson
Edna Perkins
Gitta Perl
Carl Pomerance
Ann Popkin
Than Porter
Kay Prickett

Catherine Quinn

Peter Rabinowitz
Deborah Rand
Marilyn Rapley
Peggy Reimann
Ron Ridenour
David Riley
Wally Roberts
Margaret Rose
Tom Rowe
Susan Ryerson

John Sawyer
Florence Sayer
Nancy Schiffelin
Gretchen Schwarz
Linda Seese
Phil Sharpe
Terri Shaw
John Shetterly
Ellen Siegel
Lew Sitzer
Mildred Smith
Nancy Smith
Douglas Sorenson
Charles Sowerwine
Lawrence Spears
Virginia Steele
Jane Steidemann
John Stevenson
Ruth Steward
Charles Stewart
Robert Stone
John Strand
Howard Stromquist
Richard Swanson

Morton Thomas
Eleanor Tideman
Heather Tobis
Roy Torkington
Karen Treusch
David Trimble

Bernard Wasow
Tom Watts
Judy Werner
Grenville Whitman
Christopher Williams
Edwin Wilson
George Winters
Gloria Wise
Sylvia Woog
Larry Wright

Michael Yarrow
Judy York

214

Other SIGNET Books of Related Interest

THE THIRD GENERATION   by Chester Himes

The searing novel of a woman who passes for white, and, raging against her Negro heritage, brings ruin to her family.   (#T2532—75¢)

WHEN THE WORD IS GIVEN   by Louis E. Lomax

An eye-opening account of the Black Muslims in America, and their late leader, Malcolm X. By the author of *The Negro Revolt*.   (#P2429—60¢)

SKIN DEEP   by Ralph G. Martin

A compelling and timely novel about the lives of four Negroes who seek freedom and happiness in Paris.   (#P2777—60¢)

THE PRIMITIVE   by Chester Himes

A forthright novel about a tragic love affair between two self-destructive people—a white woman and a Negro man whose lives had placed them on the fringes of society.   (#P2595—60¢)

NATIVE SON   by Richard Wright

The stark, moving novel about a young Negro's self-destructive efforts to find freedom through acts of violence.   (#T2598—75¢)

GO TELL IT ON THE MOUNTAIN   by James Baldwin

The brilliant first novel by the author of the bestseller, *Another Country*. Set in New York's Harlem.   (#P2272—60¢)

THIS IS MY COUNTRY, TOO   by John A. Williams

The observations of a sensitive, sophisticated American—who is also a Negro—as he traveled through his native country.   (#P2744—60¢)

IN WHITE AMERICA   by Martin B. Duberman

Text and supporting documents of the moving off-Broadway play about the American Negro's centuries-old legacy of pain and discrimination.   (#P2758—60¢)

WILLIE MAE by Elizabeth Kytle

Lively, poignant, often comic—the true story of a remarkable Negro woman's life as a servant in the Deep South. (#D2418—50¢)

RUBY McCOLLUM by William Bradford Huie

The famous story of a Florida murder trial in which a Negro woman was convicted for slaying a prominent white man—the father of her child. (#P2600—60¢)

INVISIBLE MAN by Ralph Ellison

A novel of extraordinary power about a Negro man's desperate search for his identity. Winner of the National Book Award. (#Q2722—95¢)

BLACK BOY by Richard Wright

The grim autobiography by the author of *Native Son,* describing the bitter yearnings of a Southern Negro for the freedoms forbidden him. (#T2341—75¢)

A MAN CALLED ADAM by Les Pine and Tina Rome

A portrait of a cynical Negro jazz musician, a man worshipped for his genius and hated for his arrogance. An Embassy Pictures release starring Sammy Davis, Jr. (#P2968—60¢)

THE SANDBOX and THE DEATH OF BESSIE SMITH by Edward Albee

Two explosive off-Broadway hits, one about a scathing domestic tragedy, the other baring the ugly circumstances surrounding the death of a great Negro blues singer. (#P2339—60¢)

UNCLE TOM'S CHILDREN by Richard Wright

Searing short stories highlighting the Negro's desperate flight for survival in the Deep South, by one of our greatest Negro writers. (#P2363—60¢)

TO OUR READERS: If your dealer does not have the SIGNET and MENTOR books you want, you may order them by mail enclosing the list price plus 10¢ a copy to cover mailing. (New York City residents add 5% Sales Tax. Other New York State residents add 2% plus any local sales or use taxes.) If you like our free catalog, please request it by postcard. The New American Library, Inc., P. O. Box 2310, Grand Central Station, New York, N. Y. 10017.